ALONE
Orphaned on the Ocean

ALONE
Orphaned on the Ocean

Richard Logan PhD
Tere Duperrault Fassbender

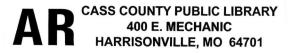

TitleTown Publishing

Green Bay, Wisconsin

Orphaned on the Ocean

TitleTown Publishing, LLC
P.O. Box 12093 Green Bay, WI 54307-12093
920.737.8051 | titletownpublishing.com

Cover design by Mike Stromberg
Interior layout and design by Erika L. Block
Edited by Julie Rogers

PUBLISHER'S CATALOGING-IN-PUBLICATION DATA:

Logan, Richard D., 1942–
Alone : Orphaned on the Ocean / Richard Logan, Tere Duperrault Fassbender
Green Bay, Wisc. : TitleTown Pub., c2010.

p. ; cm.

ISBN: 978-0-9820009-7-7
Includes bibliographical references and index.

1. Survival after airplane accidents, shipwrecks, etc. – Personal narratives.
2. Victims of violent crimes – United States – Psychology.
3. Survival skills. I. Fassbender, Tere Duperrault. II. Title.

G530 .L64 2010   2010926099
910.4/52--dc22   1005

Printed in the USA by Thomson-Shore
first edition ♻ printed on recycled paper
10 9 8 7 6 5 4 3 2 1

Never Forgotten:

Mom, Dad, Brian, and René; Gammie; Mo and Unk

For the Future:

Brooke, Blaire, and Brian; Alison, Wesley, and Arthur

–Tere

Contents

ACKNOWLEDGMENTS

by Tere Fassbender

As I sit on the shoreline of Lake Michigan, I listen to the whitecaps tumbling and crashing on the beach. I scan the horizon and think about the captain and crew of the ship, *Captain Theo*. I want to thank them for saving me from the ocean.

I thank Dr. Franklyn Verdon for being at my side when I awakened from a coma and for nursing me back to health.

Jenny Duperrault, my grandmother, I thank you for being everything to me in those first years as my gentle and loving soul mate.

Thank you Mo and Unk (Aunt Dot and Uncle Ralph Scheer) for taking me into your family and loving me as your daughter. Greg, Jeff, and Dan, I appreciate you for accepting me as a part of your family.

As my journey through life continued, I'd like to thank the Brebner family and, especially, Pam for giving me friendship in those vulnerable years.

I am so grateful to my Aunt Lois and Uncle Fritz Duperrault and cousins David, Cheri, Alan, and Jean who have always loved me and have shown interest in me throughout my life.

I would like to thank my Nebraska family for all of their love and for allowing me to be who I am.

Thank you Aunt Janet and Uncle Bob Scheer for our special times, and Victoria for always being my best friend.

ALONE

I don't believe I would have made it the last thirty-five years without my children Brooke, Blaire, and Brian. The love I have for them is unexplainable and different from the love many parents feel for their children as they are truly all I have. And now that the next generation has arrived, I am so fortunate to be a part of the lives of my grandchildren Alison, Wesley, and Arthur.

Thank you, my Ronald, for all of your love and support. You have been so good for me. You are my best friend, my safe harbor, my confidante.

I appreciate Richard Logan for all of his time and effort in working with me and writing this book. Thank you, Dick, for helping me through difficult times.

There are so many people and pets that have helped me along my rugged path. I give you a special thanks and I believe you know who you are. I am truly blessed and thankful for all who have come into my life and have helped me in some way. It is now my hope to help others by telling my story.

ACKNOWLEDGMENTS

by Richard Logan PhD

The first person I need to thank is the subject of this story, co-author of this book, and – most important – subject of a remarkable life. With characteristic courage, Tere Duperrault Fassbender was determined that her story not only be told, but that it be told honestly, warts and all. I am deeply honored that my friend entrusted her story to me, but also grateful for the example of courage, honesty and decent humanity with which she has lived her life.

Equally determined to see this remarkable story told was Tracy Ertl of TitleTown Publishing, Green Bay, Wisconsin. She shepherded, cajoled, encouraged, and capably coordinated every detail of the production of this book. All-in-all, Tracy was the gentlest of bulldozers. TitleTown's Assistant Publisher Christine Ertl, who helped her mom multi-task, knows the truth of that image better than most. Profound thanks also go to the rest of Tracy's magnificent team: TitleTown Publishing's talented Editor Julie Rogers, who understood how to improve the writing without losing the authors' voices, and how to gently make suggestions that enriched the story; Counsel Ellen Kozak, an accomplished, award-winning author in her own right, who was fierce in ensuring thoroughness and accuracy and stepped in to help with editing, thus significantly improving the book (It is great to see a publishing company with editors who actually edit!); Erika Block, who designed and formatted the interior of the book and has given it just the right look; interns Katie Stilp and Jessica Engman, who checked facts, diligently pursued missing details, formatted pictures, and supported the effort in many other ways. Everyone put in long hours. We all vowed that once the book was done, we would go on a retreat.

Although information for this book was gleaned from many sources over many years, I am especially indebted to the late Ben Funk for his research into the life and military career of Julian Harvey in 1961 and 1962. Funk, who died in 1982, also wrote some of the early Associated Press wire service stories on the *Bluebelle*.

At some point, Ben entrusted his files on the *Bluebelle* and Julian Harvey to his good friend, the late Gene Miller, Pulitzer Prize-winning *Miami Herald* writer. He evidently hoped that Mr. Miller might one day write a book. Miller gave me Funk's research notes in 1992. He had followed Tere's story and had deep affection for her, and she for him. I believe it was his hearing of my personal friendship with Tere that led him to give me these notes. Mr. Miller also showed me his own writings on the *Bluebelle*, and he helped me gain access to *Miami Herald* archives. I am deeply indebted to him. He died on June 17, 2005.

I also need to thank Hope Mercier, former secretary in the Human Development Department at the University of Wisconsin-Green Bay, for cheerfully and skillfully typing the drafts of this manuscript more than fifteen years ago that ultimately became part of this book.

I owe a large thanks to Sidney Vineburg, former rabbi of temple Congregation Cnesses Israel in Green Bay, for his intelligent conversation about the *Bluebelle*, and for his own research efforts into the case. Yes, the rabbi is also a private investigator!

There has been no greater believer in this story than Mike Blecha, retired reporter and editor for the *Green Bay Press-Gazette*. He continued to keep the story before the public and has always been a strong supporter of Tere. Along the way he was also a mentor of our publisher Tracy Ertl. Mike reiterated recently that Tere Duperrault was the bravest person he ever met.

Finally, I owe much to the student who more than twenty years ago told me "there is someone I think you should meet." I regret very much that I do not remember his name, but he helped enrich my life. Perhaps he will read this book and contact me again so I can thank him properly for introducing me to Tere Duperrault Fassbender.

I want to thank a lot of people who have been supportive, encouraging, and understanding. First, my wife, Carol, who has been dealt a bad hand herself in recent years but still plays her cards bravely and with skill, determination, and love. Our two sons, David and Jon, accomplished professionals and talented writers, both of whom have given their parents the greatest gift parents can ever receive: they have grown up to be good people. They are outshone only by our two bright and beautiful granddaughters, Beatrice and Rowan. The inspiring memory of my extraordinary mother, Edith Simmons Logan, and her example of living life with verve and humor despite chronic illness and pain, is always with me. She died far too young, but inspired many with her uncomplaining endurance and her defiant laughter in the face of adversity over many years. I need also to thank my remarkable father, Rev. Wesley Logan, also a man who loves words and uses them well. He lost the love of his life nearly thirty years ago, but he remains whole, positive, and sharp at ninety-three, and is loved and respected by many, especially his great-granddaughters. There are many other relatives and friends (such as the gang at Caribou Coffee), but they know who they are, and Acknowledgments are not supposed to be as long as the book.

I need to offer one additional thank you: to my friend Les Stroud, Discovery Channel's *Survivorman* to thousands. I am grateful to him for taking the time while in the field doing his survival thing to read this book and write the Foreword for it. I admire Les for doing with such dedication what I, an academic, have mostly only written about. But then, those who can, do.

Finally, I am blessed to have met and been profoundly inspired by some extraordinary people through studying those who have survived the impossible, Tere Duperrault Fassbender first and foremost. I am indebted to her and to many former POWs, pilots, sailors, soldiers, mountain climbers, adventurers, political prisoners – but mostly to the legions of ordinary people thrown by fate into Hell who found the hero within themselves in order to survive. Take my word: They came out better people than the rest of us, and there is much they have to teach us.

FOREWORD

by Les Stroud

I was first introduced to Richard Logan during my days of intensely studying wilderness survival. I was a relative newcomer to these skills and although there were already a few books dealing with the psychology of survival, it was Logan's first book, also titled *Alone* (Stackpole, 1993), that got to the heart of the matter, in a manner far superior to anything I had read. Eventually I would take the concept of solo survival, along with the lessons I had learned from *Alone*, to their very literal end. I would place myself twenty-three times in forced solitude, in far remote areas, for the sake of producing my television series: *Survivorman*. Among the stories in Logan's first book, the most gripping was a brief account of Terry Jo Duperrault.

Now Richard Logan has, with her help, written her full story. Part perfect Hollywood script, part hard-core story of survival and part in-depth character study *Alone: Orphaned on the Ocean* is a gripping read. Terry Jo, a young, seemingly fragile and gentle fair-skinned girl, is the embodiment of the phrase "will to live." Much has been written about the forces that enable survival: survival knowledge, luck, fitness level, and survival kits. However the single most important factor that I always land on is the "will to live." When you have no knowledge, when your luck has turned bad, when you have nothing to aid you and when your body and mind have been ravaged, the only thing left is your will. Terry Jo's will was cast

ALONE

in iron. The brilliance with which the team of Richard Logan and Tere Duperrault Fassbender tell the story of Terry Jo's survival – not just over days of peril but over a lifetime – immediately puts this tale in the league of the greatest survival stories of all time.

Les Stroud

Creator and host of the Discovery Channel television series *Survivorman* and *Vanishing World*, author of *Survive! Essential Skills and Tactics to Get You Out of Anywhere – Alive.*

PREFACE

The information for this story comes from a variety of sources:

(I) A lot of it is collected from hundreds of accounts of the *Bluebelle* case in newspapers and magazines, mostly written in the immediate aftermath of the event and researched by this author between fifteen and twenty years ago, followed up more recently via Google, the Internet, and through genealogy and records sites. Some of these accounts were in collections in the Local History section of the Brown County Library in Green Bay, Wisconsin, which has an extensive set of clippings and microfiche because of the strong local interest in the story. Some accounts were also found at the Miami-Dade Public Library in 1992, where there was also strong local interest. With the notable exception of stories written by veteran reporter Mike Blecha of the *Green Bay Press-Gazette* in 1994 and 1999, none of these sources ever had the advantage of talking extensively with Tere herself, however, and none of them went into the past life of Julian Harvey in any depth. Most of these public accounts recounted Coast Guard hearing testimony, interviewed acquaintances of Julian Harvey or witnesses in the Bahamas, or interviewed police or Coast Guard investigators.

(II) Parts of the story come from two sets of documents:

• Transcripts and records of Coast Guard inquiries, testimony, and interviews regarding the *Bluebelle* case. I was able to read the entire Coast Guard report in Miami in 1992, and the entire set of testimony transcripts and investigative reports. I also was given a copy of the summary of the report; and

• Records of extensive research and interviews by the late Ben Funk, distinguished Associated Press reporter and staff writer based in Miami. He was the one investigative journalist who dug extensively into the past life, relationships, and military career of Julian Harvey and who sought out people who had known him, including his past wives. Most of his research was done in late 1961 and early 1962. He, along with some other journalists, interviewed a number of people who either witnessed the *Bluebelle* and its passengers in the Bahamas, or who interacted with Julian Harvey before or shortly after the events described in this book. Funk passed away in 1982, and this author is fortunate to have been given his files in 1992 by his good friend, the late Gene Miller, Pulitzer Prize-winning writer and reporter for the *Miami Herald*. Gene Miller himself was also a source of some information, as he followed the *Bluebelle* story closely and was the lead writer in a series of ten-year "Where are they now" follow-ups on the *Bluebelle* story. Incidentally, Gene Miller's obituary pointedly mentioned the *Bluebelle* story as one of the most memorable stories of his distinguished career. Miller was both a consummate professional and an old-fashioned gentleman who was deeply moved by the story of the young Terry Jo and showed her both concern and kindness. I know Tere counted him as a friend.

(III) Recollections either written down or obtained by extensive interviews with Tere Fassbender, née Terry Jo Duperrault, conducted periodically over many years. Tere also supplied copies of journals she had written occasionally beginning in the 1980s. Tere was also the source of a great many news clippings about the *Bluebelle* story, as members of her family had collected many of them in the months after the *Bluebelle* tragedy.

(IV) Notes from a sodium amytal interview of Tere Fassbender conducted in 1999 by Dr. Edward Orman, highly respected psychiatrist then practicing in Green Bay. Sodium amytal is a so-called "truth serum" used to aid recall of past life events, especially traumatic ones that might have been repressed.

(V) Examination of National Oceanographic and Atmospheric Administration weather records for information on winds and currents for the Bahamas for the middle of November 1961, as well as weather records kept at the Seventh District U.S. Coast Guard Office in Miami.

(VI) Discussions with several doctors and physiologists about the progressive effects of dehydration and exposure over a period of days. I particularly want to credit my late friend and colleague Dr. Joseph Mannino, a first-rate human physiologist in the Human Biology program at the University of Wisconsin-Green Bay.

(VII) Conversations with members of the Miami police force in 1992, particularly in the Records Division, their names regrettably lost some years ago.

ALONE

(VIII) Interviews with retired Coast Guard officers Robert Barber and Ernest Murdock, principal investigators on the *Bluebelle* case. Barber was interviewed in Miami in 1992; Murdock, in San Francisco in 1999, where he was actively engaged as a volunteer on a San Francisco fireboat, continuing to serve.

Editor's note: The name Duperrault is pronounced –awlt. The name Tere is pronounced exactly the same as the name Terry. The reason for the name change is explained in the text.

CHAPTER ONE

Sailing Dreams

November 13, 1961, Monday

In the middle of the broad and deep Northwest Providence Channel in the Bahamas, the lookout on the Puerto Rico-bound oil tanker *Gulf Lion* spots a strange sight: a small, wooden dinghy, its sails furled, with a life raft tied to it. The ship draws nearer, and those on board can see that there is a man in the dinghy, and something else, something they can't quite make out, in the life raft.

Hailed by an officer on the deck of the ship, the man calls out, "My name is Julian Harvey. I am master of the ketch *Bluebelle*." Then he adds, "I have a dead baby here. I think her name is Terry Jo Duperrault."

This is the first inkling the world will have of the fate of the *Bluebelle* and the disappearance of the five members of the Duperrault family who had chartered her for a dream cruise through the Caribbean. In fact, the "dead baby" in the life raft will turn out to be seven-year-old René Duperrault. Her sister Terry Jo will be found days later and many miles away, clinging to life and to a small cork-and-canvas float. She is alive only because of her own determination, an eleven-year-old alone on the vast open sea.

ALONE

It had long been the dream of Arthur Duperrault to take his family sailing on the azure seas of the tropics. Looking out on the chill blue waters of Lake Michigan, the optometrist from Green Bay, Wisconsin, recalled the warmer waters to the far south that he had sailed during World War II, and spoke often of wanting to live for a year on a sailboat, cruising around the world from port to port, island to island. He had served in the Navy in the Pacific and had learned to love the sea. Even years after the war, with a busy career, a wife, and three children, he still held this dream.

By 1961 he had become successful enough to fulfill that dream, at least in part. He knew he could afford to take his entire family of five on some kind of a sea cruise. Despite their comfortable life in a prototypical mid-century, middle-western city, he wanted to give his family something more, the gift of a glimpse of tropical paradise.

That family included his wife Jean, his son Brian, then fourteen, and his two daughters, Terry Jo and René. That year, instead of facing a hard Wisconsin winter, they would head south to fulfill their father's dream.

~~~~~

Arthur Duperrault had always been a leader, and a success. He had been president of his senior high school class, the class of 1939, at Green Bay West High School, where he'd been a debate champion. After high school, he went on to Lawrence College (now Lawrence University) in Appleton, Wisconsin.

With World War II underway, Duperrault dropped out of Lawrence in 1942 to join the Navy. At only five feet eight inches in height, and slight of build, he had to build himself up and gain weight before the Navy would accept him. Working out would become a life-long habit; in later years he was very concerned about keeping physically fit and spent some part of every day at the local YMCA.

After basic training, Duperrault was assigned to the Far East, where he served as a medical corpsman on the recently built Burma Road, the supply line from the British colony of Burma to the interior of China during the Second Sino-Japanese war.

It was on the voyage to Burma that this young man from the "frozen tundra" of Wisconsin found that he loved being on the ocean. The ocean is different from the "inland sea" that is Lake Michigan – the salt sea smells different from the fresh waters of that Great Lake, the fish that inhabit it are different, and Lake Michigan, even in summer, never warms to the temperatures of tropical waters. And the ocean goes on forever, whereas you are never more than a few hours from shore on even the largest of the Great Lakes.

Arthur Duperrault spent long hours on the deck of his transport ship, leaning on the rail and staring into the far horizon. Once in Southeast Asia, he traveled with the allied forces chalking up long distances on rugged trails, by horseback and on foot, treating men for malaria and dysentery as well as for wounds incurred in deadly jungle fighting with the Japanese invaders. More than once, he found himself in mortal danger. Witnessing the horrors of war up close, he never failed to acquit himself well, as commendation letters from his superiors attested. Once, when allied forces linked up with Chinese troops in the jungle near the border with China, he had the opportunity to meet the Chinese leader, Chiang Kai-shek.

After twenty months in the Far East, with the United States

ALONE

by then at war, Duperrault was assigned to duties in Washington, D.C. In February of 1943, he volunteered to go to China as a medic, serving there for most of that year. He was then assigned to the Pentagon in late 1944. While there, the quiet red-haired pharmacist's mate met the dark-haired, vivacious Jean Brosh of Madison, Nebraska, who was working as a secretary at FBI headquarters in Washington, D.C. After the kind of quick courtship that became common during the war, they married in Washington in December of 1944, Arthur in his dress uniform and Jean in a dark, satiny dress (from their black-and-white wedding photo, one cannot tell its color).

Duperrault was discharged in November 1945, and he returned with Jean to his home in Wisconsin. By 1947 he and Jean had started their family with son Brian. The family lived with Duperrault's parents in De Pere, Wisconsin, just south of Green Bay, while Arthur commuted to the Northern Illinois College of Optometry. He drove south to Chicago for classes during the week and returned to spend weekends with his family until he graduated in 1949. He then returned to Green Bay to practice.

Determined to build a good life and raise a family in security and abundance, he worked hard and became so highly regarded by his colleagues as a competent, innovative professional that he was soon a leader in the Wisconsin Optometry Association. He also prospered in his optometry practice because he had taken the risk of selling the latest vision product, the contact lens, and the gamble had paid off.

Green Bay was a blue-collar city surrounded by dairy farms with a robust economy built on cheese manufacturing and the busy paper mills that lined the Fox River. It was a town where rugged

German-, Belgian-, and Scandinavian-Americans made a good living in those mills. It had always been one of the better-known small cities in America, but not just for its remarkable work ethic and healthy economy. It happened to be the smallest city in the United States that had an NFL team, and the football team had won a string of NFL championships in the 1930s and one in 1944.

Although the Green Bay Packers hadn't done well for the past two decades, they had started to win again in 1959 and 1960 under their new coach, the no-nonsense if not-yet-legendary Vince Lombardi, who believed that winners were the guys who worked the hardest. A blue-collar team for a blue-collar town, by the fall of 1961 the Packers were racking up a string of wins. Soon, Green Bay would again be synonymous with toughness and grit, and with the little guy defeating the big guy.

Terry Jo Duperrault, her older brother Brian, and younger sister René grew up in a white stucco house on an acre of wooded ground near the tenth green of the Shorewood Country Club just outside of Green Bay. Living on the east shore of the bay of Green Bay, the Duperraults were just a few miles northeast of the city. They lived not so much in a suburb as on the edge of the country-side, as there were many farms nearby and few other houses.

Their father often spoke of his experiences during the war and of his dream to sail the seas. Both his wartime adventures and his sailing dreams were the stuff of many of the bedtime stories he told his children. He wanted them to appreciate adventure and realize that "travel is the best education."

With her dark brown hair and dark brown eyes, Jean Duperrault was attractive to the point of being stunning. She was slender and stylish, with an independent streak: she had two very close girl-friends with whom she went many places and attended a number of activities, unusual in an era when married women were expected to socialize as their husband's appendages.

An energetic homemaker who worked hard to make her family's life both secure and beautiful, she was also an enthusiastic gardener. Her adventurous streak came out in her meal planning; serving her family exotic foods like pigs' feet, avocados, and fried green tomatoes reflected that.

Jean took art lessons and the artist in her turned their recreation room into an Asian room for entertaining. She decorated it with paintings and artifacts that Arthur had brought back from the Far East. Both she and her husband wanted their kids to know there was a big, wide world out there.

The Duperraults were all athletic and loved the outdoors. Dr. Duperrault ("Doc" to many of his friends) and Brian won many father-son golf matches at Shorewood. Jean, too, was an avid golfer. She would sometimes stay behind to play golf with her girlfriends in the summer while her husband took the children to the beach. She was good enough at the sport to win the club's Vice President's Golf Cup in 1960; her enthusiasm for it was reflected in the fact that she was elected president of the Shorewood Club's women's organization.

Doc developed a love for handball and soon became a highly ranked player, winning thirty trophies in state competitions. In early 1961, paired with a good friend, he won the state handball doubles championship.

Arthur and Jean Duperrault were not just living the post-war good life, they were solid citizens firmly ensconced in the American middle class. They were both active in civic, school, and church affairs, attending the small Presbyterian church in nearby Wequiock. Doc won a YMCA leadership plaque as the top layman volunteer in the Y's physical fitness program. He served a term as president of the Green Bay Jaycees and earned recognition as a national leader of a Jaycee program to support shut-ins. And for six years, he was the volunteer clerk of the Wequiock Elementary School, just north of their house, which the children attended. Dr. Duperrault was fit and athletic and meticulous about his appearance. He had wavy red hair and blue-grey eyes, and wore a suit to work every day. His shoes were always highly polished. A very sober man, it was difficult to get a smile out of him. Clearly he took his responsibilities seriously.

Having survived the terrors of the Burmese jungles, he was no stranger to risk and danger. He once received national publicity when he spent hours digging out the family collie, Ching, who had fallen into a ten-foot-deep trench. He won local attention on another occasion when he dived, fully clothed, into the cold waters of Green Bay to rescue the daughter of a good friend who had slipped through a life ring.

As hard-working, strong, and capable as Doc Duperrault was, he also was an involved and caring father. He was often the one who nursed the childhood cases of poison ivy, sunburn, and the flu. When Terry Jo came down with the flu and slept on the couch, which she often did when she was little, it was her father who made her tea as soon as he got home from work. But Doc Duperrault wasn't the only one good in emergencies.

Jean, the farm girl from Nebraska, was, too. Twice when her tomboy daughter Terry Jo injured herself and needed stitches, Jean stitched the cuts herself. She also drove a neighbor to the hospital on treacherous roads during one of the roaring blizzards for which northern Wisconsin is still famous.

And Doc was an avid sailor, especially experienced at ice-boat sailing during the frigid Wisconsin winters. This was a risky, unforgiving, high-speed sport that demanded great skill. The boats often reach fifty or sixty miles per hour, and sailors wore very little crash protection. Dr. Duperrault also had several friends who owned sailboats large enough for extended sailing excursions in summer, and he learned how to sail these larger sailing craft on such trips. He also sailed small Lightning sailboats on the bay with his children and friends.

Brian, the oldest Duperrault child, was, at fourteen, a freshman at Preble High School in Green Bay. He was small for his age – Terry Jo was taller than her older brother – and other children had taken to calling him "Shrimp." He took offense at that, so he attended judo classes at the YMCA and, like his father, was very muscular for his size. Brian was outgoing and loved to play baseball as well as golf.

Except for his blue eyes, Brian resembled his mother's side of the family – and played the piano, clearly having inherited his mother's musical talent. Jean Duperrault was an accomplished harmonica player. He was also, like his mother, quite artistic. Some of his drawings won ribbons at the local fairs. But Brian also loved to build things and spent hours in the woodshed next to the house that doubled as a workshop. He built a go-cart that all of his cousins enjoyed, and engaged in chemistry experiments that often caused small explosions.

Seven-year-old René, unlike her two blonde siblings, had dark brown eyes and brown wavy hair. She was very feminine, preferring to wear dresses rather than play clothes. She was a quiet child, and always shy, even with family members. Even at her young age, René already had all of her adult teeth. Unfailingly good-natured, she seemed always to have a smile. She loved her dolls, playing dress up, and playing with the neighbor children. Her happiness was one barometer of how secure and loved all of the Duperrault children felt.

From left, Brian, Jean, Arthur and René Duperrault

ALONE

Terry Jo, the middle child and older daughter, was tall and slim and, like her little sister, quiet. At age eleven she was two or three inches taller than her brother, who was physically a carbon copy of his slightly built father. Like everybody else in the family, she was a strong swimmer, and she also liked ice skating, water skiing, and horseback riding. She did not particularly enjoy social and group activities and was content to be the loner in the family.

Unlike the rest of the family (except for René), she couldn't stand golf, and preferred to stay home to watch her little sister or play by herself rather than getting out on the golf course. In summer she was always a tanned and sun-bleached platinum blonde. She found time to do a lot of reading and had a B average in sixth grade at Wequiock Elementary School. She also spent summers on her maternal grandparents' farm in Nebraska, riding horses and helping tend the animals, especially calves and baby pigs.

Terry Jo loved animals and kept several rabbits, two dogs, and five cats at home. She was constantly bringing home stray dogs and other wild creatures. These included a wild dog named Sandy that no one else in the family could get near. She started a pet cemetery and planted flowers on the graves of her deceased pets.

Terry Jo's world was so secure that, like a lot of other middle-class kids in the 1950s, she had to invent her own adventures and had to pretend that real dangers existed. She loved to wander alone in the woods near her home and play dramatic jungle-survival games, building her own little forts in various secret places, stocking them with supplies. Her favorite spot was hidden in a space between bushes that was open only to the afternoon sun. She would seclude herself there in the late afternoons, enjoying feeling both adventurous and secure at the same time.

She would pretend to hide from enemies who she would spy on from the thicket. (Usually the "enemies" were merely golfers on the next-door golf course.) Even though she played with Barbie dolls and had a large doll collection, her idol was Tarzan. She loved watching old Johnny Weissmuller movies on TV, so much so that she even made herself a Tarzan-inspired fur loincloth using skins of rabbits and squirrels that she had found dead in the woods, which she sewed onto an old bathing suit. She wore this as she prowled the woods on her secret jungle adventures and when she swung on vines in her own private jungle.

By 1960 Doc realized that he had become so busy that he was losing contact with his children. He decided that if he didn't take his family on that dream sailing cruise soon, it might never happen. The time had come. He had decided the family needed first to try out a brief sailing excursion to see how well they would adapt to the routine of sailing and to being together in the confined space of a sailboat. He subscribed to yachting magazines and read the ads of sailboat brokers. He collected an extensive file of yachts for sale, all of them large, ocean-going boats capable of extended cruises for a family of five. In the summer of 1961, he found someone to take over his optometry practice for a year.

There was no problem getting the children out of school for at least the fall semester. Their teachers said they could study during the trip and should have no trouble keeping up with their classmates. Their mom would be their tutor. So they packed up their things and headed for Florida, caravanning in two station wagons, the larger one towing a small hardtop trailer that they could all sleep in during the trip.

The plan was that they would spend at least the fall trying out life at sea, and extend the sabbatical to a whole year if all went well. The family actually had been to Florida for winter vacations twice before and loved it. They had all enjoyed days at the beach, swimming in the surf, and fishing from piers. They had not, however, all sailed together.

And so, after a brief stop at a trailer park on the Gulf Coast near Tampa, the Duperraults – planning to take a one-week "shakedown" cruise through the Bahamas – found their way to the *Bluebelle*, tied to a mooring in Fort Lauderdale's Bahia Mar yacht basin.

The *Bluebelle* was a ketch, a two-masted sailboat with a sixty-foot-tall mainmast toward the bow and a shorter forty-five foot mizzen mast toward the stern. Originally built as a racing yacht, the boat was long, low, and narrow. The combination of its simple linear design, low profile and white color made it elegant and sleek. Fully rigged, the *Bluebelle* usually carried three sails: a mizzen, a mainsail and a jib forward of the mainsail. On the *Bluebelle* the mizzen mast was right at the front of the large cockpit, which had benches along the sides for passenger seating. The steering wheel was at the rear of the cockpit.

The boat was sixty feet long overall, or about forty-five feet at the waterline, and fifteen feet wide at its broadest point. In front of the eleven-foot-long cockpit was the twenty-one-foot-long cabin roof covering most of the interior of the boat and rising two feet above the deck. Normally the ship's white wooden dinghy and black rubber life raft were stowed along the left side of the cabin roof, and a white five-man cork life float was lashed to the right forward cabin roof. On either side of the cabin were walkways that were not quite two feet wide and were bordered at the deck edge by stanchions that held a cable safety line about thirty inches above the deck.

The Bluebelle

The largest area inside the boat was the thirteen-foot-long main cabin, finished in blonde wood and illuminated by three round portholes high up on either side and a skylight in the roof. The main cabin contained seating and a settee in the dining area that converted to a double berth along the left side. There was a small "head" with a shower and toilet in the right front corner, and a kitchenette along the right side. The main cabin was accessed from the cockpit through a companionway off to the right side of the mizzenmast. It led to steps down into the cabin.

There was also a small sleeping cabin underneath the left side of the cockpit that was about nine feet long and six feet wide. It was mostly taken up by a four-foot-wide sleeping berth and had storage lockers on the outer wall, at the rear of the cabin, and under the berth. The sleeping cabin extended from the rear end of the main cabin back toward the stern. Just on the other side of the interior wall of this sleeping compartment was the engine room. Most of the rest of the space under the cockpit was taken up by the engine room compartment.

In front of the main cabin, accessed through a door next to the bathroom, was the main bedroom, which was about eight feet long. It was mostly taken up by a queen-size bed, a couple of chairs, a dressing table and lockers, under the bed and on the walls, for storage.

Separated by the wall at the front of the main bedroom was a forward cabin accessible only through a large covered passageway on the forward deck that was the same height as the main cabin. The bottom of the mainmast was housed in the wall between the main bedroom and the forward cabin. This forward cabin was about ten feet long, plus there were two berths that formed a V-shape as they extended forward along the hull to the point of the bow. This was the crew cabin for the skipper and his wife.

The *Bluebelle* was designed to carry five or six passengers comfortably in the main bedroom, main cabin (on the convertible double berth), and aft sleeping compartment – perfect for the five-member Duperrault family.

The *Bluebelle*, coincidentally enough, had been built in 1928 in Sturgeon Bay, Wisconsin, only an hour north of Green Bay in Door County (the Wisconsin peninsula that extends into Lake Michigan). Originally named the *Lady Jane*, it had sailed the same waters of Green Bay and Lake Michigan with which the Duperrault family was familiar, before it was sold several times and ended up in Fort Lauderdale.

CHAPTER TWO

The Adventurer

Not a lot was known about Julian Harvey's earlier life when he was hired in 1961 as skipper of the charter sailing yacht *Bluebelle*. Everyone knew that the handsome forty-four year old was a retired Air Force lieutenant colonel and a veteran bomber and fighter pilot. But it wasn't at all unusual that little was known about someone new to Fort Lauderdale. Like a lot of other Floridians, Harvey had moved there only after retiring. What everyone had heard was that during his nineteen-year military career, he had received both the Distinguished Flying Cross and the Air Medal for actions as a B-24 bomber pilot in World War II, and he had flown the charismatic F-86 Sabre Jet in the Korean War. It was also known that Harvey loved to sail.

After retiring from the Air Force in 1958, the former fighter pilot (at the time either divorced or merely separated, but certainly holding himself out as unattached) cut quite a figure. When he came first to Miami and then to Fort Lauderdale to pursue his long-time dream of becoming the full-time master of a sailing yacht, he became a regular at local marinas and yacht clubs, rarely bothering to talk with men, but always seen at the bar with a beautiful woman.

He briefly owned his own seventy-foot schooner, the *White Swan*, which he sailed out of Miami a number of times on charters through the Bahamas. And he had owned at least one other large sailing yacht some years earlier when stationed at Eglin Air Force

Base on the Gulf Coast of Florida. He sold the *White Swan* after about a year, possibly for financial reasons, but he loved sailing so much that he even worked briefly as a deckhand on the majestic four-masted windjammer *Polynesia*. Determined to be at least a sailing-yacht master, he signed on to be charter skipper of the *Bluebelle*, owned by Harold Pegg, in the summer of 1961.

Not only was Harvey the most dashing of figures, even at age forty-four, the former jet jockey still more than looked the part. Straight from central casting, he looked the ideal of the heroic fighter pilot: movie-star handsome with a shock of blond hair and a broad, boyish smile. He was so handsome, in fact, that it was rumored that years earlier he had worked as a male model. In addition, he was sophisticated, well-mannered, and extremely charming.

Before going to college, Julian Harvey worked as a male model for the Powers agency.

To top it off he was a fitness buff decades before fitness became the rage. He worked out often to keep the hard, lean body that gave women still more reason to be attracted to him. When he worked on his boat in the Bahia Mar marina, or when he posed for photographs, he usually managed to do so with his shirt off. The only flaw in Harvey's gorgeous persona was an occasional stammer – which only seemed to make this Adonis more human and accessible – and a mild case of lazy eye.

To the chagrin of many ladies in Fort Lauderdale, the attractive playboy married a beautiful former TWA flight attendant and aspiring writer on July 26, 1961. Mary Dene Jordan – Dene to her friends – was coincidentally from Wisconsin, like the *Bluebelle* and the Duperrault family, another denizen of the Dairy State to coalesce on the *Bluebelle*'s final voyage. It was rumored that Dene was just the most recent in a long string of Harvey's wives, but no one knew for sure.

Mary Dene Jordan was a TWA flight attendant before she married Julian Harvey in the summer of 1961.

CHAPTER THREE

A Brief Time in Paradise

By Wednesday morning, November 8, 1961, the *Bluebelle* had been provisioned for a week's trip. The Duperraults eagerly went aboard to begin their highly anticipated voyage. The children were romping on the deck, excited about the adventures ahead, when Harold Pegg, the *Bluebelle*'s owner and Harvey's employer, came aboard to take on a supply of ice. He later recalled that Brian was carrying a .22-caliber rifle.

"What are you going to do with the gun?" Pegg asked.

"Shoot some sharks," the boy said, laughing. In 1961 the idea of shooting at sharks and considering it sport was far more acceptable than it would be today.

Once the Duperraults and all of their gear were on board, Pegg went ashore and Brian hurried to help Captain Harvey cast off the lines. The *Bluebelle*'s 115-horsepower Chrysler engine rumbled softly as Harvey slowly turned the wheel and the boat gradually pulled away from the dock, wisps of exhaust sputtering from the stern. The engine changed to a deep-throated, muffled roar as the captain powered the boat east toward the mouth of the harbor. From the shore Pegg watched as Harvey reached open water, slowed and turned the *Bluebelle* into the southeasterly wind, idling the engine and running up the sails. As her sails filled, the *Bluebelle* almost appeared eager to fly as she leaned with the wind and began to gather speed as she headed east into the southeasterly wind as close as she could manage, a practice sailors call tacking.

Glistening under a new coat of paint, the sleek yacht drew admiring glances as she sailed gracefully from the dark waters of the harbor into the green of the open sea, and finally the deep blue of the Gulf Stream, the mighty river in the sea that passes between Florida and the Bahamas as it pounds northward along the entire East Coast. The Florida coast faded behind them and then they were alone with the breezes and the gulls on an empty ocean. Over the horizon ahead, the seven hundred islands of the Bahamas archipelago basked in 72,000 square miles of sun-washed seas, holding the promise of fulfillment of Arthur Duperrault's dream and of adventure for his family.

Before the *Bluebelle* slipped out of sight of shore, a gray squall appeared on the horizon creating a patch of gusty, swirling darkness on the water that raced towards the vessel. Winds running before the storm made the *Bluebelle*'s shrouds (cables supporting the masts) sing and churned up the Gulf Stream. The squall passed quickly, but the wind continued to blow at a steady eighteen knots – about twenty miles per hour – and the sea was covered with breaking whitecaps. The *Bluebelle* rose and then plunged and shivered slightly from the tension of wind versus wave as her bow sliced through eight-foot swells.

As she sailed nearly into the wind with her rigging taut, the wind lifted the white spume off the tops of the waves and threw it into the faces of the ketch's passengers. The tropical wind was refreshing and the salt spray breaking over the bow was cold and exhilarating. In the excitement of it all, nobody cared about getting wet or getting the first taste of salt on their lips. Their great adventure had begun.

Terry Jo and Brian, after admonitions from their mother to be careful, straddled the bowsprit – a plank extending forward from the bow – alternately bending far forward to watch the bow slice through the waves and then leaning defiantly into the wind and spray, grinning as they scanned the expanse of sea ahead of them.

Allowing for the northward drift of the Gulf Stream, Captain Harvey set his course as close to southeast as he could, sailing into southeasterly winds towards Bimini, the nearest of the Bahama Islands, some fifty miles away. Bimini was, in 1961, one of the world's most famous big game fishing centers, and here the Duperraults planned their first island visit.

But the rough crossing of the Gulf Stream took longer than expected, and by the time Bimini's palm-clustered waterfront came into view, it was five o'clock. The customs office had closed for the day and Harvey was unable to present his papers for entry into the British-governed Bahamas, so the party was forced to remain aboard the *Bluebelle* overnight. Once they were cleared at their first point of entry, they would have free access to all of the islands.

When dawn broke Thursday in a blaze of pinks, golds, and blues, the Duperraults were already on deck to see their first show of life in a tropical paradise. On the island, pelicans flapped their great wings sleepily and rose on the wind to soar out in flawless formation to find breakfast. They glided gracefully, surprisingly close to the crests of the waves, until they sighted small fish under the sun-sparkled surface. Then the great birds zoomed upward, turned, tucked in their wings, and dived, slicing cleanly into the water with surprising force. In a moment they returned to the surface, gulping down their prey while they shook their heads to fight off pesky gulls. Then with beating wings throwing off sprays of salt water, they returned to the air to hunt again.

Out to seaward, beneath a flock of sea gulls, a school of big, powerful tuna so numerous they formed a great gray cloud in the green water, fed on baitfish. The gulls dived and scuttled over the surface, fighting over the scraps. Along the Bimini beach, other gulls stood like sentries in formation at the water's edge, waiting for whatever delicacies might wash ashore with the next wave. As the water receded, the gulls hopped to pick up tiny shellfish swept ashore by the waves. As the next wave broke, it erased their sharp three-pointed footprints from the wet sand. After each scramble for morsels in the surf, the birds turned into the southeast wind and allowed it to dry their outstretched wings and smooth their feathers.

For unknown reasons, although the ketch was seen just offshore, Harvey did not go ashore at Bimini Thursday morning to present his papers. Instead, he hoisted anchor and was seen moving out toward the northeast. The wind was still strong and he drove the *Bluebelle* under engine power for several hours toward Great Isaac Cay, a tiny islet rising forty feet out of the sea, with a red and white banded lighthouse to warn travelers of the area's dangerous shoals. In the protective lee close to the west side of Great Isaac, they spent their second night at sea. The next morning they sailed the deep Northwest Providence Channel due east toward the village of Sandy Point on the southwestern tip of Great Abaco Island, a large island that runs north to south on the eastern edge of the channel.

In the choppy waters of the channel, the sea offered never-ending entertainment to the family from Wisconsin. Flying fish leapt from the surface and soared like birds for incredible distances. A giant sea turtle swam on the surface close to the *Bluebelle*. The fin of a sleek shark cut the water, and the Duperraults marveled at the thought that beneath was an unknown world full of both beauty and danger. Porpoises breached near the boat, bounding and twisting through the waves like so many playful school children.

After crossing the channel, the *Bluebelle* entered the gentle and impossibly clear emerald shallows of the Great Bahama Bank and a world far removed from northeastern Wisconsin. Here, in 1961, a sailor could roam for weeks on end, dropping anchor each night in a perfect harbor, seldom seeing a human face.

The sea was wild with color from horizon to horizon, like a stained-glass window. The colors of the water changed constantly. Over deep channels, the water was deep greenish-blue like the open ocean. It was light blue at ten to fifteen fathoms, light green at four to five fathoms, pale green at one to two fathoms, clear and colorless as tap water at less than a fathom, and foamy white where it broke over the coral reefs. Where the bottom was rocky, the light blues changed to dark green, and where the light green waters flowed over a grassy bottom, it took on a brownish tinge.

Eleven-year-old Terry Jo, the most outdoorsy and keenest observer of nature in the family, took in all of these things.

Most of the tiny islands dotting the sea were uninhabited, with some of them offering gently curving beaches as beautiful as any in the world. Some were dazzling white and some were pale pink, covered with sand that was actually finely ground coral. The entire Bahamas, in fact, are a nearly two-mile-high mound of carbonate built up out of what once was living coral laid down over millions of years.

When a harbor was too shallow for a ship with the *Bluebelle*'s six-foot draft, Captain Harvey anchored in the lee of the island and the party went exploring in the ship's dinghy. They rowed or sailed the little craft ashore to comb deserted beaches, possibly the same beaches once visited by pirates when they raided Spanish merchant ships laden with treasure from the New World. Even today, beachcombers sometimes turn up doubloons or pieces of eight.

Over the next couple of days, using facemasks and snorkels, the Duperraults paddled through the shallows of two or three islands, admiring the underwater rainbow of multi-colored tropical fish and undersea gardens. Used to the fresh water of the Great Lakes, they enjoyed being remarkably buoyant in the crystal salt water. Terry Jo paused in one of her swims to stand in the shallow water and look toward the *Bluebelle* where she lay anchored farther out in the water. Self-conscious in her new bathing suit and her changing body, Terry Jo saw that Captain Harvey was staring at her from the deck. It made her uncomfortable for just a moment, but she soon forgot and went back to swimming.

All the Duperraults except René were powerful swimmers who easily learned the arts of snorkeling and spearfishing. Sometimes, they went in the dinghy to explore the reefs, while Mrs. Harvey and René would play on a beach, collecting shells and digging in the sand.

A large fleet of two-masted schooners and single-masted sloops crowded the harbor at Sandy Point, and sailing craft rode at anchor at moorings offshore or were beached for overhaul and repair. The town lived entirely off the sea, and fishing boats and trading sloops constantly came and went. As Harvey anchored the *Bluebelle* fifty yards offshore, the air was filled with the snapping sounds of the wind whipping slackened canvas, and the squeal and rattle of blocks as sails were lowered.

Except for exploring some beaches, this was the first time the *Bluebelle* party had gone ashore. In the colorful settlement of modest huts clustered on sandy ground in the shade of a huge palm grove, the Duperraults explored and chatted with the locals. Dr. Duperrault was so delighted with what he had seen that he told village commissioner Roderick W. Pinder he planned to build a vacation home at Sandy Point.

"This has been a once-in-a-lifetime vacation and we have thoroughly enjoyed it," he told the commissioner. "We are going to come back and use Sandy Point as a winter resort."

Jean Duperrault, the amateur artist, was enchanted with the village, its small homes painted in bright pastels and surrounded by multi-colored flowers and shrubs.

Harvey presented his papers at the commissioner's office for formal entry into the British-owned islands, not having had the opportunity earlier. Technically he was late doing so, and it was a strict requirement, but the easy-going regime of 1961 Bahamian authorities generally allowed such lateness as long as boats simply didn't come and go at will, and they generally did not make an issue of American boats dropping anchor off their beaches to swim and explore, as long as they did register in good time.

Harvey picked up a supply of fresh water while members of the party mailed letters, to be delivered to the Bahamas capital,

Nassau, on the regular weekly run of the small sloop that plied the islands, running the mail.

In one letter, Mrs. Harvey complained to her mother, Mrs. Laura Dene Jordan – who, like the Duperraults, also lived in Wisconsin – that she was never able to be alone on the ship or the beaches. "I think I'll devise some kind of disappearing act," she wrote. "Why, oh why, can't people leave me alone? At this point, I'm ready to shoot myself." She added that she didn't like getting up at dawn to cook breakfast for the party.

But Dene's mother said her daughter might have been speaking in mock exasperation, for her tone was otherwise cheerful and the letter was signed with an impish smiley pumpkin face. Mrs. Harvey wrote that the Duperraults were "lovely people" and that the children were well behaved. It was, however, the first time in her letters home that she made no mention of her husband.

Coming out of the commissioner's office, Julian Harvey encountered Napoleon Roberts, a local fisherman and old acquaintance. They had sailed together briefly some years earlier on the windjammer *Polynesia* shortly after Harvey sold the *White Swan*. Harvey was deck hand and Roberts was cook and waiter. As they reminisced, Harvey said he missed fresh crawfish. Roberts promised to catch some that night and Harvey invited him to come aboard the *Bluebelle* that evening. Roberts said later that everyone on board seemed relaxed and content. He noticed that Harvey and his wife were drinking, but the Duperraults were not.

On Saturday morning, maneuvering the *Bluebelle* with its six-foot draft through rocks and reefs along the shallow banks, Harvey set course eight miles northwest to Gorda Cay, a tiny island with a small settlement and a beautiful white horseshoe beach in a picturesque harbor. Off the island, the *Bluebelle* party was observed trolling for game fish, the ketch moving steadily under power.

Early Sunday, the *Bluebelle* was back at her anchorage off Sandy Point and the Harveys reappeared at the commissioner's pink stucco office in the afternoon to fill out the forms for leaving the Bahamas and returning to the United States.

Dene chatted with the commissioner's wife and told her that another charter had been arranged and "we'll be back before Christmas." She volunteered to bring clothing and magazines for the locals on the next trip. The commissioner and his wife were impressed with her charm and cheerfulness. Harvey was jovial, and laughed and joked with his wife.

On the beach, Dr. Duperrault talked with another local fisherman, Jimmy Wells. Doc told Wells about a huge shark that had been trailing the *Bluebelle*. Wells recalled that Doc said he had considered shooting at it with his rifle, but then thought better of it, although Brian had been excited about the idea. Duperrault invited Wells aboard the *Bluebelle* and the party gathered around Jimmy while he told stories of his fabulous Abaco Island. He told them of the terrific fishing and about the great, green jungle in the island's interior where wild boars, dogs, and horses roamed. They were descended from domestic animals that escaped a century ago from a ship that had piled up on the reef. Over time they had turned wild and multiplied. There were even feral chickens that had learned to fly again and lived in the trees.

"Everyone on the *Bluebelle* was nice and having a wonderful time," the fisherman said afterward. "It was a happy ship."

ALONE

The young fisherman was invited to remain for dinner and, with the others, ate chicken cacciatore and salad prepared by Mrs. Harvey in the galley. It was to be the last meal ever served on the *Bluebelle*.

The next day the tanker *Gulf Lion* spotted the *Bluebelle*'s dinghy towing its rubber life raft. Strangely, it seemed to some that the man in the dinghy initially made no effort to signal them, but as the *Gulf Lion* turned and approached, he was seen waving. Harvey then identified himself and told them that he also had the body of little René on board, although he initially had misidentified her as Terry Jo.

Harvey told the *Gulf Lion* crew that he was the sole survivor of a tragedy. In the middle of the previous night, a sudden squall had dismasted the boat, causing the mainmast to plunge down through the ship, holing the hull. The mainmast also pulled the mizzen mast down into the cockpit over the engine room. The damage was so extensive that gas lines in the engine room ruptured, causing the ship to erupt in flames as it slowly sank, a jumble of tangled rigging on its deck. Many of his passengers, who were in the cockpit, were injured in the violent collapse of the masts and rigging. Harvey said he had managed to clamber forward, launch the dinghy and raft, and dive overboard but that everyone else was trapped on board by tangled rigging and fire in the cockpit, or had jumped overboard into the night. After the boat sank he was only able to find René, the youngest daughter, floating face down in her lifejacket.

The captain of the *Gulf Lion* immediately called the Coast Guard, pursuant to long-standing agreements with the then-British Bahamas, to report the loss of the *Bluebelle*, an American craft. The Coast Guard launched an extensive air and sea search for any survivors or remains of the lost ship, also apparently permitted by the agreement provided U.S. Coast Guard boats stayed outside of a three-mile area around the Bahamas.

The *Gulf Lion* took Harvey to Nassau, the largest city in the Bahamas, which was about sixty miles to the south. Harvey, having been given $180 by the sympathetic crew of the *Gulf Lion*, flew back to Miami the following day. Upon arrival, Harvey also called the Coast Guard and was asked to appear two days later, on Thursday, November 16, for an inquiry into the loss of the *Bluebelle* and the death of presumably all on board.

CHAPTER FOUR

A Captain's Tale

At 9 a.m., November 16, Lieutenant Ernest L. Murdock convened what was to be a routine Coast Guard investigation into the loss of the *Bluebelle*. He and Coast Guard Captain Robert Barber were to be the chief investigating officers, although Barber was not present as the hearing began.

Harvey seemed in good spirits when he walked into Murdock's tiny fourth-floor office in the Calumet Building in the Miami business district, surprising to many since his wife was presumed dead and, as captain, he bore at least some responsibility for the apparent deaths of the entire Duperrault family. He was dressed neatly in a brown sports jacket, brown slacks, and a tan sports shirt.

The handsome captain exchanged cordial greetings with Harold Pegg, the *Bluebelle* owner and his employer, and flashed a broad smile when he was introduced to others in the room.

Before the interrogation began, Harvey pressed Murdock for news of the Coast Guard search for survivors and wreckage from the *Bluebelle*. He now seemed nervous, and his life-long stuttering problem that seemed to reappear under stress or fatigue was now evident, but Murdock considered this a "natural reaction to his ordeal."

The lieutenant telephoned the Search and Rescue branch of the Coast Guard and then informed Harvey that the search thus far had been entirely fruitless. No other survivors and, strangely, not one single trace of debris from the lost vessel had been sighted by searching planes and ships.

Harvey exhaled heavily as he sat down in a straight-backed wooden chair at the corner of Murdock's desk, while Pegg and his attorney took seats in the rear of the room. The young lieutenant, speaking softly, explained that the purpose of the inquiry was to determine the cause of the *Bluebelle*'s loss and whether any incompetence, misconduct, or law violations contributed to the disaster. Then he placed Harvey under oath and asked him to give his account of what happened. That account would be dutifully recorded in the official transcript of the hearing.

"Do you want the full story?" Harvey asked.

"Definitely," Murdock replied.

The officer leaned back in a swivel chair and scratched notes on a pad as Harvey began to explain. Unknown to many at this time, the *Bluebelle* incident was actually the third time in the past six years that Harvey had lost a ship. This time, however, he had lost his passengers, too, and he had a gripping tale to tell.

The following is excerpted from Julian Harvey's testimony.

Harvey began by explaining that he and Dr. Duperrault had planned a two-day sail to cover the two hundred-mile route back to Florida, sailing both day and night with a couple of breaks of only a few hours.

Harvey: "We set sail from Sandy Point on the east side of the Providence Channel shortly after dark Sunday night. It was our intention to stop for a few hours in the lee of Great Stirrup Cay,

get three or four hours of sleep, then proceed to Great Isaac, anchor
in the lee for a little more sleep, then reach Fort Lauderdale Tuesday night or Wednesday morning.

"When we left Sandy Point, the weather was good. There was a fresh breeze coming up, about fifteen knots. At night, I always travel with reduced canvas. I had the staysail up and the mainsail up. I did not have the mizzen or the flying jib up. Under this sail configuration, the *Bluebelle* could easily carry twenty-five or twenty-eight knots of wind without heeling over uncomfortably. She could carry more than that. In other words, that was a very safe, conservative sail plan.

"There were a few small rain squalls in the area. We encountered one of them about halfway between Sandy Point and Great Stirrup Cay. Because it had been such pleasant sailing, with no power on, everyone was in the cockpit. It was a big, roomy cockpit. The children were there with some minor bedding and were napping.

"Then this small squall hit us and a monstrous thing happened. In a twenty-knot wind, the mainmast failed one-fourth or one-third of the distance above the deck. It was not a failure of stays; it was a failure of the wood in the mainmast. A fifty-foot length of the mainmast came hurtling straight down, piercing the deck like it was made of paper. It was just like a telegraph pole going straight down on the deck. It tore through the one-inch white pine of the deck and continued on down through the bottom of the hull. As it gained momentum, the stays from the mainmast to the mizzenmast gave a gigantic pull to the mizzen, breaking it in at least two places. The mizzenmast collapsed among us in the cockpit. This collapse of the entire rig reduced us to a bare hull wallowing in the sea."

A ketch like the *Bluebelle* has a taller mainmast forward toward the bow and a shorter mizzen mast aft. These masts are held upright and supported by strong cables that run from high up on the masts to the edges of the deck of the ship (shrouds). These support the masts laterally. There also are strong cables (stays) that run fore and aft from the mast tops to the bow and stern, and from one mast to another. These support the masts longitudinally.

All of this interconnected rigging is under a great deal of tension, especially when under pressure from the wind, so a collapse of a mast could conceivably pull everything down, including the other mast. The sudden release of tension also could cause a violent whipping of cables that would tear at anything and anyone on the deck as well as at other parts of the rigging, causing splinters and the like to fly. All of that rigging, plus spars and huge, heavy pieces of the masts themselves, mean that a great tangle of heavy debris could indeed fall violently onto the deck.

Harvey's stutter was getting worse now. There were long pauses as his jaw quivered and he reached for words but found it difficult to say them. As he continued, he shifted in his chair and sometimes reached up to run sun-browned hands through his blond hair. It was clear that he was under great strain. That was understandable, considering what he had just gone through and that his wife was among those presumed dead, not to mention the entire Duperrault family.

Harvey's testimony continued:

"Fortunately no one was hit directly by the falling mizzen, but my wife and Dr. Duperrault were cut on the legs by splinters.

"I was steering at the time and I started the engine and left it at slow ahead to give us control. I briefly checked the wounded and told everybody to sit fast and not to panic, that I was going forward to get the cable cutters and get rid of all the cables around us. I ran forward, clearing my way through the debris, went below in the forecastle, and finally got the cutters.

"Emerging from the forecastle forward, I saw that a fire had started in the cockpit area, and because the wind was down the deck, fore to aft, the six passengers were moving aft, away from the flames (onto the fantail, the small section of deck to the rear of the cockpit). I seem to remember them taking some of the boating cushions aft with them. The children already had on their life preservers.

"As they were standing on the rear deck (the fantail, behind the cockpit), very close to the gasoline tanks (located under the rear deck), I was naturally in deadly fear of an explosion. I ran below, picking up two five-pound fire extinguishers.

"The water was already a foot deep in the hold, coming through the hole made by the mainmast. The boat was wallowing and the water was rushing backwards and forwards, making it hard to maintain footing."

Back on deck, Harvey testified, flames were shooting up through vents in the cockpit from the engine room. They had enveloped the cockpit, then spread quickly across the deck, which had been freshly painted with highly flammable neoprene. He said he emptied the small extinguishers on the flames with little effect. Now the boat was beginning to sink, and he decided to launch the dinghy and rubber life raft that were stowed forward on the port side of the top of the main cabin.

Harvey: "The passengers astern could see me doing this, and they apparently decided among themselves to jump overboard and wait for me to get the boat back to them rather than stand there facing the fire in that area. They had confidence in me. I cut the rail with the cable cutters, bent the stanchion, and managed to launch the loaded sailing dinghy without swamping it.

"I could hear faint yells, although we were going into the wind and they were downwind of me.

"I tied the raft and dinghy together and rowed to the stern. It was pitch dark and I could see nothing in the water. I had a carbide water light, but it didn't work and I threw it overboard."

Harvey added that the *Bluebelle* was going down fast now and he said he shouted until he was hoarse, but no sounds came back to him out of the blackness of the night except the sounds of the wind and waves and rain. At last, he came upon little René but she was dead, floating, he said, face down in the water.

Harvey: "By this time, the *Bluebelle* had gone down, very quietly. As she sank, the fire went out. There was never a huge general fire, just in the cockpit and stern areas.

"I was so exhausted, it was all I could do to get the little girl up in the life boat. I tried artificial respiration on her."

Harvey was beginning to repeat many of his statements. Speaking of the discovery of René, he said, "I pulled the child's body into the raft. I pulled her in. I did it myself."

And he stressed, over and over again, how exhausted he was because he had had to lower the dinghy and raft without aid.

Murdock eyed him intently.

Harvey: "The sea was building up. I tied the little girl's body in the rubber raft. By myself. Then I must have stayed in the area two hours before giving up hope of finding the others. After that, we drifted until about six thirty in the morning. I still kept shouting.

"It was cold. At daylight, I opened the emergency rations. I could see that I was faced with a problem. The wind was from the southeast and I was afraid that I might drift into the Gulf Stream (roughly fifty miles west) and on north. So, from the first, I rationed the food.

"The sun came out and warmed me up, but I was continually doused by the waves. The sea by that time was up in the neighborhood of eight-, nine-, or ten-foot combers, and the wind was a steady twenty knots. The tops were hissing.

"About 1300 hours I saw a large steamer coming directly toward me, about five or six miles away. At three miles distance, it veered off to my left and missed me by at least a mile. However, I was told that one man on the stern saw me. They turned, came back alongside and picked me up.

"They fed me and treated me for mild shock, radioed the Coast Guard in Miami immediately, and proceeded to put me off at Nassau."

When Harvey had finished, Murdock sat for some time staring at the ceiling, his expression stony. Some things didn't add up. He found Harvey's twice saying that he did things "by myself" to be odd. If he was so obviously all alone, why did he keep adding unnecessary emphasis to that fact? Murdock wondered if Harvey was trying to cover for somehow having contributed to the deaths of his passengers through negligence. But, perhaps, he was just feeling guilty because, as skipper, he was responsible for his passengers' safety.

The serious, black-haired lieutenant also wondered how a mast could pierce a deck as Harvey said it did. In his experience, broken masts didn't plunge straight down. Pushed by the wind that broke them, they tumbled over the side, carrying the shrouds and stays with them. It also was strange that when the fire broke out, the passengers stayed aft when they might have been able to struggle forward, just as Harvey had done.

Also, if the *Bluebelle* had caught fire, as Harvey said, why didn't the lookout on the eighty-one-foot-high Great Stirrup Cay lighthouse, only a few miles away, spot the blaze on a dark night? And why didn't Harvey, supposedly an experienced seaman, once in the dinghy hoist sail and take the dinghy to the nearest island such as Great Stirrup Cay, only a few miles to the southwest, instead of sitting there worrying about whether he would drift into the Gulf Stream, and whether his food would run out? A southeasterly wind would have been a very fair wind for making it to the southwest and Great Stirrup Cay with its light to guide him. Instead it seemed that he had traveled due west.

Yet, there was no evidence to counter his story, and no known reason to be suspicious of someone reputed to be as reliable as war hero Julian Harvey. All that stood on the negative side of the ledger was that Captain Barber was personally aware of a previous incident where Harvey had lost another ship, but it had been judged to be an accident, not Harvey's fault, and no lives had been lost.

Finally, Murdock turned to Harvey and began his interrogation. First, he asked if Harvey had attempted to call for help by radio.

"When the mainmast went, it took the antenna," Harvey replied.

Murdock: "You made no attempt to use the radio?"

Harvey: "I knew it wouldn't work. I didn't even attempt it. It would have been a waste of time."

Murdock: "Didn't you have any flares?"

Harvey: "I did have flares in the emergency kit in the raft, but they were way down in the kit and they weren't easily available. Frankly, I didn't think of them at the time."

The fact that Harvey didn't dig for the flares in such a desperate situation and, further, that he "didn't think of them" was flabbergasting to Murdock. Everyone knows about flares. Even the greenest sailor would quickly think of them and find the energy to poke around in a bag, much like a homeowner seeing a grassfire would think of his garden hose and grab it, even though he was not a trained firefighter. Murdock found Harvey's explanation preposterous. And yet there was no evidence of anything sinister. And Harvey had just survived something extraordinarily trying, even for a war veteran.

When Murdock asked why he had not hoisted the sail on the dinghy, Harvey explained, "The wind was too strong and I was too exhausted during the night. In the morning it would have been swamped because I was towing the life raft. The dinghy (by itself) could have done fairly well, but with something in tow it would have gone under or over, the wind was so strong."

He added that he was afraid that if he hoisted the sail in the morning, the lookout on any passing ship might have figured that he was just out for a pleasant sail and ignore him. Not having sails up also seemed peculiar to Murdock, as the first priority in that situation is to be seen, and a white sail is far more visible than a naked mast on a low-lying dinghy. Harvey also knew these waters well and was an experienced sailor, and would presumably have wanted to be heading toward a safe port somewhere. A sail also enables a craft to make way in the water, which, however slow the progress, is much more stable and less conducive to seasickness than simply wallowing in the waves.

On the other hand, Murdock conceded, trying to make headway by raising sail in a dinghy towing the dead weight of a raft would be tantamount to the dinghy pulling a heavy sea anchor, meaning that a wind of any strength would tend to push the dinghy over rather than propel the tandem forward. So Harvey could have been right.

Murdock: "Now, this carbide water light which you threw overboard, did you pull the plug on it?"

Harvey: "I could see nothing to pull. I'd been told that all you do is put it in the water. I just threw it overboard."

Murdock looked stunned. This piece of equipment was simple to use and entirely familiar to most sailors of large seagoing craft. A carbide water light was a lamp with two chambers: an upper one that contained water, and a lower one that contained chunks of calcium carbide. Allowing water to drip slowly on the carbide produced the flammable gas acetylene, which burned brightly enough to be a standard seaborne emergency light until recent times as well as a much-used lamp for mining and spelunking. The seaborne carbide water light was ignited by a plunger with a steel head striking a flint and creating a spark.

The plug mentioned by Murdock released the water onto the carbide, and was easy to see. Murdock looked at the experienced sailor and past owner of big sailboats, a highly experienced combat veteran skilled in how to keep his head in emergencies, and a skipper who was required to be schooled in the use of emergency, safety, and rescue equipment. Murdock was astonished that Harvey said he simply threw something as vital as the carbide emergency lamp overboard.

"Captain," he asked, "how much experience do you have in sailing a craft of this type?"

Harvey sat upright and said, indignantly, "I have owned and operated craft of this type since 1954. I've sailed extensively in the Bahamas."

So Harvey, by his own account, was an experienced sailor. This made aspects of his story even more difficult to comprehend.

Harvey went on to say that when the mast fell, he started the engine and turned into the wind with just enough forward speed to keep the *Bluebelle* from wallowing and hold her at a speed of three-quarters of a knot. He remained at the wheel just long enough to "tell the people to calm down" and then gave the wheel to Arthur Duperrault. The doctor was bleeding, he said, but the wounds were superficial and, "I knew he could hold it until I got back with the wire cutters."

Murdock: "Who else was bleeding besides the doctor?"

Harvey: "My wife. I'm certain she was bleeding. I don't remember if the others were bleeding, but they may have been."

Another Coast Guard lieutenant rose to ask Harvey if Duperrault, at the wheel, actually kept the *Bluebelle* into the wind after the fire broke out. If there were no fire, the young lieutenant said, this might have been good seamanship. At a time like this, however, it would have forced the flames back on Duperrault and his family and driven them into the sea. In other words, even the simplest instinct would lead one to turn the wheel away from the wind and flames.

Harvey may not have known it, and, at the time, the Coast Guard evidently did not either, but Dr. Duperrault was no greenhorn sailor. As noted earlier, he had sailed craft of various sizes on Green Bay and Lake Michigan. He knew full well how to handle a sailboat, even a larger one. What's more, he had gone through Navy training. And he had also proven himself more than once to be a very cool head in a crisis.

"Yes," Harvey said. "The others had moved aft, away from the fire, but the doctor held the vessel on the course I had given him until he abandoned it and went back (onto the fantail) to jump overboard with the others."

Harvey continued, saying that Terry Jo, Brian, and René were wearing life preservers, and there were two life rings on the ship's rails aft. He said he believed the adults had grabbed these when they jumped. There were two other life rings on the rails forward and he threw them overboard, he said, hoping those in the water would find them.

Murdock: "Was everyone awake at the time of the accident?"

Harvey: "Everyone was awake. The little eleven-year-old girl was screaming. I tried to keep her quiet. She probably had a nightmare or something. She didn't know what was going on. She woke up and wasn't wildly hysterical but with a little bit of shock."

During the night, while he drifted with a dead body at his feet, Harvey said he could see the reflection of the Great Stirrup Cay light in the sky. When the *Gulf Lion* picked him up, he was only five miles from the lighthouse.

A few more routine and technical questions were asked, and then Harvey was dismissed. The examiners called Harold Pegg to testify.

Murdock told Harvey he could remain to hear Pegg's testimony, and to cross-examine if any statements conflicted with his own story.

A moment later, Captain Barber rushed into the hearing room with startling news.

CHAPTER FIVE

The Sea Waif

While Harvey was telling his story to the Coast Guard three days after he had been rescued, and four days after the *Bluebelle* had last been seen, Nicolaos Spachidakis, second officer of the Greek freighter *Captain Theo*, was scanning the waters of the Northwest Providence Channel. The freighter was passing through the channel bound from Antwerp, Belgium, to Houston, Texas, and Spachidakis was on watch. From his post high up on the bridge, he could see several other ships scattered over the sea.

By some odd chance, one of the thousands of tiny dancing whitecaps in the distance caught the officer's eye. It didn't seem to disappear like the others. For no particular reason, he continued to watch the tiny and unrecognizable speck, squinting through the sun's bright glare. At first he discounted it as a piece of debris; then decided it must be a small fishing dinghy because he could just make out a small bump that might be a fisherman. Then he realized with a start that no tiny fishing dinghy could possibly be out that far. He summoned Captain Stylianos Coutsodontis to the bridge.

When first sighted, the object was about a mile away off the starboard bow. As the ship drew closer, they were stunned to see that it was not a dinghy, but a small, white, oblong life float. Incredibly, sitting on it, alone in a vast emptiness of sea, was the last thing that could possibly be there: a beautiful, blonde-haired girl. She was looking up and waving feebly. They stared in stunned amazement, as if a female Moses had just been delivered up to them from the bulrushes. The sight challenged first perception, then comprehension. Where had she come from?

The girl was reclining stiffly, leaning back on her arms, wearing pale pink pedal pushers and a white blouse, her feet dangling over the side of the float. One of the crewmen took a picture of her looking up from her tiny craft, squinting against the sun, dwarfed by the expanse of empty sea around her. Her bleached hair was glowing brightly in the sun above her emaciated and painfully drawn sunburned face. This picture would shortly be wired around the world, and front pages everywhere would proclaim the miracle of the "sea waif." The picture was so powerful that it became a two-page spread in the next *Life* magazine: one page showing her on the raft, the other showing nothing but empty water. Ironically, it was printed in the very same issue that told of the disappearance of Michael Rockefeller, the son of New York Gov. Nelson Rockefeller, in the sea off of New Guinea. He had been lost trying to swim ashore from a native canoe.

The captain called out orders to stop the engines and to put a small raft over the side. He was afraid that if one the ship's large and unwieldy lifeboats were used, it might hit the child's light float and knock her overboard. The men quickly lashed some empty oil drums together and lowered the makeshift raft over the side.

Suddenly, the captain shouted orders to hurry. Sharks, perhaps attracted by the commotion, or maybe they had been stalking her for who knew how long, were circling the little float and moving in closer to the girl's dangling feet. Crew members crowded the rails and shouted to the girl not to jump.

Evangelos Kantzilas, a crew member, quickly sculled the unwieldy craft over to the float and lifted the girl aboard. She fell limp in his arms. He pulled back alongside the ship. Another crewman at the bottom of a pilot ladder slipped a bowline under the child's shoulders and she was hoisted, hanging limply on the rope, a couple of stories up to the deck.

Her lips were puffy, her skin badly burned, her cheeks sunken, her hair bleached almost white by the tropical sun, and her eyes were dull and unseeing. A seaman lifted her and stood her on deck but her legs buckled. She was clearly severely dehydrated and in desperate shape. Coutsodontis picked her up gently and carried her to a spare cabin where she was placed in a bunk. Sea-hardened Greek sailors, with tears in their eyes, crossed themselves as they looked on, speechless. Moments later they tenderly gave her sips of water and fresh orange juice, gently sponged the salt from her fiery-red body with damp towels, and put Vaseline on her cracked lips.

The captain tried to get her to talk, but she did not respond and her eyes gave no sign that she saw or heard him. He kept coaxing and pleading, but she was mostly comatose, and he feared she was too far gone – from what kind of an ordeal he could barely imagine.

"Can't you tell me your name and how you found yourself in the water?" he asked. "I want to report to the Coast Guard that we have found you. If you will tell me your name, I can send information to your relatives that you are still alive."

Finally, she shook her head weakly and gestured downward feebly with her thumb, indicating in the captain's mind that she must be the sole survivor of some kind of disaster at sea that had claimed the rest of her family.

"You can't be sure they are lost," he said. "Maybe some other ship saved them."

She shook her head weakly again, and again she pointed to the water. She seemed to be saying that she had seen them swallowed up by the sea. A single word, "*Bluebelle*," barely rasped from her dry throat and through her swollen lips.

"Do you have any relatives anywhere?" the captain asked.

She nodded and he bent over as she whispered "yes" in his ear. She then managed to tell him hoarsely that her name was Terry Jo Duperrault and that she had relatives in Green Bay. Then she slipped back into unconsciousness.

The Coast Guard had not specifically alerted Coutsodontis to be on the lookout for *Bluebelle* survivors, but he had overheard commercial news broadcast telling of Captain Harvey's rescue. He had paid little attention to it, though he was aware that he was in the general vicinity where the *Bluebelle* disappeared.

He telegraphed the Coast Guard in Miami: "Picked up blonde girl, brown eyes, from small white raft, suffering exposure and shock. Name Terry Jo Duperrault. Was on *Bluebelle*." This was the electrifying news that had brought Captain Barber rushing into the hearing room. It was also news that overnight made Terry Jo Duperrault the most famous girl in the world.

Even if it was uncertain, apart from Harvey's not entirely credible account, what had happened to the *Bluebelle* and the Duperraults, it was now clear that Harvey was not the only survivor. Somehow Terry Jo had survived both whatever had befallen the sailboat and then four days without water in burning daytime sun and freezing nights, all the while somehow balancing herself on a life float that was about two-and-a-half feet by five feet – an oblong ring of canvas-covered cork with rope webbing in the middle that was designed to be held onto for a few hours by survivors in the water, not ridden on for days. (The *Captain Theo* did not retrieve the float, but the Coast Guard did find it a couple of days later. It had nearly fallen apart.) The float was, in fact, one that had been lashed forward on the cabin top of the *Bluebelle*. The veteran seamen of the Greek crew shook their heads in disbelief at the thought of what this young girl must have gone through.

A reply came quickly, asking for further information on the girl's condition, the position of the ship, and wind and sea conditions in the vicinity. Knowing exactly the location where Terry Jo was picked up in addition to that of Captain Harvey, the Coast Guard could now estimate more closely where the *Bluebelle* had gone down; they only needed to calculate the course on which the wind and currents would have set their crafts. This would give them a better idea where to look for debris and possible survivors, although they feared too many days may have passed. Coutsodontis replied that the girl was in a deep sleep and he hesitated to rouse her for a more thorough examination. He reported excellent weather and slight to moderate seas.

More messages came, giving him medical instructions on the care of the child. He was then told that a helicopter would arrive at the vessel at 1340 hours and he was to have her ready for transport.

The lumbering Coast Guard helicopter flew to the ship from Miami, hovered over the deck and lowered a basket, its rotor blades buffeting the air with noisy thuds. A burly crewman, blinking back tears, gently lifted Terry Jo and strapped her in, then gave the signal to hoist up. As the basket rose, she opened her eyes, managed a wan smile, and waved a weak goodbye to her saviors standing on the deck. The tough sailors waved back, still amazed by what they had seen. As the basket was drawn inside the noisy helicopter, she again dropped back to sleep.

The Coast Guard quickly determined, once they had a sense of the generally westerly course Terry Jo had drifted on, that another Greek ship, *Asian*, must have passed close to Terry Jo's float the previous midnight. An hour before the *Captain Theo* sighted her, another freighter also must have missed her by about five miles. Later, Terry Jo would relate that she did see the lights of ships at night, and other ships during the day.

"You would not have been able to see the raft at a distance of more than a mile and a half at the most from my bridge, which was fifty feet above the water," Coutsodontis said. "It was a miracle that we chanced to sight her."

But, perhaps if Harvey had forcefully insisted on a search at the time he was picked up by the *Gulf Lion*, she might have been found days earlier, for she must have been drifting no more than a mile or two east of him at the time. But, if things had happened as he said they did, she should have gone down with the *Bluebelle*. How did she come to be on that pathetic little cork float? Had she, in fact, somehow found one of the flotation devices Harvey had said he had thrown from the dying *Bluebelle* into the sea?

At Mercy Hospital in Miami, Dr. Franklyn Verdon was waiting at the landing area when the helicopter arrived with Terry Jo. When he spoke loudly into her ear, she awoke just enough to mumble her name. Then she fell unconscious again and was oblivious to the throng of news media with cameras and flashbulbs that jostled behind her from the helicopter to the emergency room.

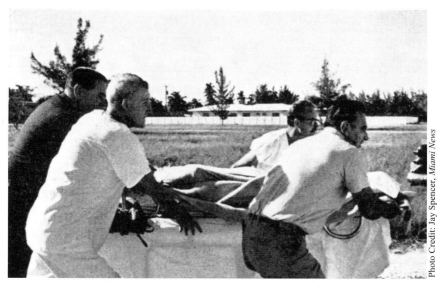

Terry Jo being rushed from the helicopter into the hospital in Miami.

Photo Credit: Jay Spencer, *Miami News*

CHAPTER SIX

A Warrior's End

"Oh, my God!" Harvey said when he heard the news of Terry Jo's miraculous rescue, echoing words of surprise uttered by the others in the room. He pushed his chair back and looked down for a moment. Then he raised his head, looked around and said, "Isn't that wonderful." Others nodded, then went back to shaking their heads as they, too, processed the extraordinary news. Harvey got up, walked to a window overlooking busy Flagler Street, and stood there for some seconds staring out.

The street below was filled with a mix of locals, newly arrived Cubans fleeing Castro's revolution, and tourists easily identifiable by their loud sport shirts. Pigeons flew about in great clusters, and men with gravelly voices solicited customers for sightseeing buses. A block to the east, the royal palms of Biscayne Boulevard waved in the soft trade wind that came in off the tumbling waters of the Gulf Stream.

When Harvey turned back from the window, he headed toward the door without a word, seeming preoccupied.

"Captain Harvey," Murdock called, "don't you want to remain for the rest of the testimony? You have that privilege."

Harvey shook his head, smiled briefly, nodded to the room, and departed. Murdock watched him go through narrowing eyelids. He and Captain Barber exchanged glances. Then they huddled. Within minutes a telephone call went out to the Miami Police Department.

The Coast Guard officers asked that a guard be placed outside Terry Jo's hospital room. They had no specific reason for this move, but Harvey's testimony had too many holes in it. They had no idea what he might have been hiding, if anything, and Terry Jo was the only person known to be alive who could corroborate or contradict his account of the *Bluebelle*'s fate.

~~~~~

The day after Harvey walked out of the Coast Guard inquiry, shortly before the noon checkout time, a maid knocked on the door of Room 17 at the Sandman Motel on Miami's busy Biscayne Boulevard. It was a hot day. Even though the street ran near the cool breezes of Biscayne Bay, the sun was baking the pavement. A stream of automobiles, bringing refugees from the first icy grip of a northern winter, rolled along the sunny boulevard. At the Sandman, guests splashed and laughed in the small swimming pool, or sunned themselves in deck chairs.

When no one answered, the maid unlocked the door of the air-conditioned room. The cool air felt good to her skin. There was a slightly odd odor as she entered the room, but she thought little of it. She was used to the smells of tightly closed motel rooms.

One of the twin beds was rumpled. As she pulled the sheets from it, she noticed a small splotch of blood on one of them. She went to the bathroom to collect the used towels, but couldn't open the door. It wasn't locked but something inside was blocking it, something large and soft seemed braced against it.

Here the odd smell was more noticeable. Suddenly nauseated, it hit her that it was the sickly sweet smell of blood. Her screams brought the motel manager. He, too, was unable to force the bathroom door open against the dead weight that was holding it. The manager telephoned police. A young patrol officer responded and reached the scene at 12:14 p.m.

The strong young officer put his shoulder to the bathroom door and shoved. It gave a little, then sprung back. He shoved again, harder, and forced it open just far enough to stick his head inside. A blood-covered body was sprawled face up on the tiled floor. The officer looked into the dead face of the man who had apparently slashed himself, with his blank eyes, and reacted in stunned amazement.

"That's Julian Harvey!" he exclaimed. The officer had previously been a Miami harbor patrolman, and had known the handsome charter-boat captain well, or as well, perhaps, as a great many people thought they did.

The police were quickly able to reconstruct that when Harvey had abruptly left the Coast Guard building the previous day, he had gone to his car parked on the street nearby, removed a suitcase, then left his car there and waved down a cab. He had checked into the motel about 11 a.m., registering as "John Monroe" of Tampa. He had gone upstairs, carrying the suitcase and a small, brown paper bag. He had not been seen again by the motel staff.

From the clues in the room, it was simple for police to piece together what had happened.

Some time in the wee hours of that morning, Harvey got up from the bed. With the neatness that was apparently characteristic of him, he placed the empty whisky bottles that had been in the paper bag in the wastebasket, right side up.

Then he went over to the desk, sat down, and began a letter addressed to a friend, James Boozer, a resident of Miami. They had been together during Air Force training days. Harvey wrote of his love for his fourteen-year-old second son, Lance, and he asked that arrangements be made for the boy's adoption by a Miami family who had been watching him. He wrote with his usual clumsy scrawl, which looked more like that of an elementary school student than of a college-educated Air Force officer, and contrasted oddly with his neatness and his sophisticated demeanor.

"I'm a nervous wreck and just can't continue," he scribbled. "I'm going out now. I guess I either don't like life or don't know what to do with it."

There was no reference to what had happened on the *Bluebelle*.

He sealed the envelope. Then, almost as an afterthought he wrote on the back, "Cremate and bury at sea." After more thought, he scratched out "cremate" and underlined "bury at sea."

He placed the envelope squarely in the center of the desk and, at one side, a briefcase containing a picture album – an album stuffed with images of his life. His clothes were hung neatly in the closet; his suitcase was in its proper place on the luggage rack.

The police conjectured that first, he thought he'd kill himself on the bed. Sitting there, with his back against the headboard, he cut into a vein in his thigh with a double-edged razor blade. But as the first drop of blood stained the sheet, he had apparently decided this was not the way. He pulled on his trousers and moved toward the bathroom.

He paused and turned back toward the bed, then pulled a $10 bill from his pocket and pinned it to a pillow – something for the maid, perhaps an apology for the unpleasant messiness of it all; a final act, perhaps, of one who still thought of himself as an officer and gentleman, and wanted others to think of him that way, too.

Again, he turned toward the bathroom and, again, he paused. A bloodstain was spreading over his trouser leg. Wincing, he went to the briefcase and removed two pictures from the album, portraits of his second son, Lance, and of his wife, Dene. He carried them into the bathroom and propped them up carefully on the top of the toilet tank, where he could look at them as he sat down on the cold floor with his back to the door.

Then he finished what he had started to do. He proceeded to slash his ankles, his wrists, his forearms, his thigh (this very deeply), and then even both sides of his neck. Hardened police officers gaped in amazement at the gory scene. He was slashed so badly that deep muscle was laid open to the bone in his thigh and his body had been drained of blood. No one had ever seen so many cuts – or such extremely deep ones – on a suicide before. Most suicides who die by cutting choose the relatively gentler method of getting into a warm tub, cutting their wrists, and letting life slowly ebb away. This was unspeakably violent.

Those who saw Harvey's body could only imagine what it took to cut oneself in this manner, and to continue to do it through horrific pain. In fact, he was cut so badly that some wondered at first if he had been murdered and then a clumsy attempt had been made to make it look like a suicide. The slash in his thigh was so deep that it seemed impossible anyone could have willingly inflicted that on himself, not to mention all of the other cuts. Officers shuddered to think of a man cutting and re-cutting and re-cutting with a small blade all the way through his muscular thigh to the thighbone.

It also didn't look at all like the way someone motivated only by intractable grief would kill himself. It was too extreme, more like a scene of horrible torture. If it was a suicide, how much self-hate must a man have to inflict such a thing on himself? And, if true, why such self-hate? Questions about just who Harvey was, the *Bluebelle* disappearance, and Terry Jo mounted. Why would this man have committed suicide on the heels of the appearance of one of the *Bluebelle*'s passengers who provided a sign of hope that there might be more survivors, including his own wife?

Julian Harvey's burial at sea, as requested in his suicide note.

Photo Credit: Jay Spencer, *Miami News*

The discovery of the mutilated body electrified investigators probing the mystery of the *Bluebelle*. Had the captain killed himself because a half-dead child had returned like a ghost to confront him? But confront him with what?

His friend James Boozer offered a possible explanation. "When he came to my home after the *Bluebelle* loss, he was in a state of shock and depression over the deaths of Dene and the Duperrault family," he said. "He told me that as he sat in the lifeboat with the little girl's body, he felt that he didn't want to go on living."

The young officer who was first on the scene and who knew him also concluded that Harvey had "decided to kill himself before Terry Jo was found. He would have done it because of Dene. They were very close. After he married her, for the first time since I had known him, he seemed genuinely happy. She was the girl he had always wanted."

But although no one yet knew the full story of Julian Harvey, and no one had yet heard the story that Terry Jo had to tell, there was a second story that Harvey told Boozer that provided another version of what had happened. Perhaps it explained what Harvey was trying to hide with his dubious account.

To reporters, Boozer insisted that Harvey had made his suicide decision before the rescue of Terry Jo. Because Boozer and Harvey had been such good friends, Boozer's pleading on Harvey's behalf was given less credence. However, one night he asked Lieutenant Murdock to meet him in the study of a local church. The minister was there. Boozer asked to make a statement under oath in the presence of the minister. He was sworn in by Murdock.

What he was going to say was not easy, Boozer said. He was going to tell a story that he had sworn to Harvey he would never reveal.

"The first night [Harvey] came back from Nassau," Boozer said, "he had gone into detail with me about the accident. I asked him then when was the last time he saw Dene, and he said she was diving over the stern of the boat, along with Dr. Duperrault, as if to give aid to someone in the water. I heard his story three times, when he told it to his son, to me, and to Pegg. In its entirety, it seemed too perfect. Why couldn't he help anybody else in the crisis? There were a few discrepancies and I [had seen] a doubtful look on Pegg's face [when he listened to Harvey's account]. I was pretty much convinced that Julian was still in a bad state of shock and wasn't able to remember just what happened at the time of the accident."

Boozer continued, saying that he had asked Harvey after his testimony if there was anything more to the story.

"[Harvey] placed his hands on my shoulders and began to say over and over, 'Why did it have to be them? Why couldn't it have been me?' His voice was full of regret – and guilt. I began to think about the conflicting stories he had told and I began to press the subject, not knowing how he would accept it. He stepped over and sat down on the bed. I was still standing in the middle of the floor.

"I asked him if the strain could have been so great that he would have forgotten just what he did in the emergency. I reminded him that, more than likely, one or more of the others would drift ashore or be picked up somewhere. I told him I hoped that his story would match that of any survivor.

"I seemed to be getting to him now. I reminded him of our years of friendship, of our many sails into the islands, the Gulf Stream and the Gulf of Mexico. I reminded him that he had always confided in me and I asked him if there was anything on his mind, any feeling of guilt.

"At this point, I told him point blank, 'Julian, why don't you tell me what really happened out there? I'm your friend and I want to help you all I can.'

"He stood quickly, looked me straight in the eye, and said, 'Will you take a vow on [his son] Lance that you will never repeat what I am going to tell you?' He was stuttering the worst I had ever heard. His left eye was straight but his right eye appeared to be moving around and the eyelid batted up and down. 'When the mainmast snapped and the mizzen fell among us,' Harvey said, 'it knocked Dene and Doc overboard. I lost my nerve when I saw the blood and guts on the deck and jumped overboard, abandoning the ship. The next thing I knew I was pulling the little girl into the boat with me. Remember, Jim, you're my friend. You took a vow.'

"I asked him about the fire but he looked as if he didn't see me. He slowly sat down on the bed and laid his head on the pillow. I kept talking to him, but he didn't say a word. His eyes were closed, so I put his feet on the bed and went to my room. I felt quite relieved. I knew that he did also."

This account was dramatically different from his testimony, and it made Harvey's suicide much more plausible. It smacked somewhat of a deathbed confession. He had not only lost his beloved wife, not only lost the Duperrault family on his watch, he also had panicked in a crisis, jumped overboard like a coward, and tried to save no one. Hardly the actions of the brave and heroic warrior most believed Harvey to be. No wonder it had seemed that he had something to hide.

It now seemed clear that he was consumed not just with grief, but with remorse and guilt – and, for a military man as proud of his accomplishments and as concerned about his image as Julian Harvey, a deep and abiding shame. Was he such a proud man that such shame would have been intolerable and he had no alternative but suicide? Shame can, after all, make one want to disappear. And shame is, according to many psychologists, partly anger directed at oneself. Perhaps, then, Harvey had killed himself because, as a proud man, he had not only lost so much but had found himself so abjectly wanting in a moment of crisis. No wonder he had attacked himself so horribly in his suicide.

Once this new story started to get around, a number of observers began to think that it explained Harvey's strange account and was far more plausible than Harvey's unsatisfactory formal testimony. For many it began to give closure to the sad story of the *Bluebelle*. His friend Boozer certainly thought so.

CHAPTER SEVEN

The Dark of Night

Whatever happened on the *Bluebelle* that night on the Bahama deeps, it had driven the captain to an apparent suicide. Only one survivor now remained who might be able to make clear what actually happened once and for all, and establish which, if either, of Harvey's accounts was true.

On the second floor of Miami's Mercy Hospital, Terry Jo lay in a coma. At first, when the helicopter had deposited her at the hospital door, attendants had placed her in an airy room overlooking Biscayne Bay. But Dr. Verdon took one look out the window and ordered her transferred immediately, before she awoke, to a room across the hall, above the hospital's parking lot. With such a land-locked view, visions of sinking sailboats with bloody decks, or floating bodies, or sharks lurking near tiny life floats, are not conjured up so easily. The job of saving the critically ill child would be difficult enough without added emotional complications.

The sea orphan's heartbeat was too fast, too erratic, and very weak. Dehydration had damaged her kidney function. Her temperature was too high; her blood pressure too low. For Terry Jo, rescue was no guarantee of survival. As glucose and saline were pumped into her system to restore fluids and electrolytes to her severely dehydrated body, Dr. Verdon said it would be thirty-six hours before he could accurately determine her condition. There was the threat of massive organ failure, pneumonia, or heart fibrillation.

She had gone just about as long as a human being could go without water – four days – and still live. In fact, a person would be lucky to survive for three days on the ocean if it was hot and sunny every day. But the miracle that she was still alive testified to her toughness and an indomitable will, and the doctor said, "I believe she'll pull through."

Doctors and nurses stood watch around the clock as she lay in a coma that first day, her pretty, almost classic, features composed. Occasionally, she stirred and her tongue crept out to lick burned and cracked lips. Sometimes, her brow furrowed and her features contorted, as though a dream was taking her back to some nightmare moment on the doomed *Bluebelle,* or on the raft during four days on the lonely sea. One could only imagine what kind of dreadful moment was in her thoughts.

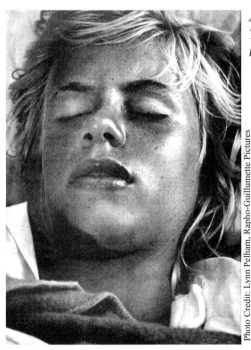

An extremely sunburned Terry Jo lies in a coma in the hospital after her rescue.

Photo Credit: Lynn Pelham, Rapho-Guillumette Pictures

But young bodies bounce back fast and on the second day she roused from her stupor. But she did not try to talk. The doctor would not have allowed her to speak of her adventure in any case – not yet, not until she was strong enough to cope with what certainly had to be tragic memories. The swelling was going out of her lips and the angry redness of her deep sunburn was beginning to fade.

"In a case of dehydration like this," one observing doctor commented, "if you don't restore the body fluids in forty-eight hours, you lose your patient." In Terry Jo's case, this was accomplished by Saturday, her second day in the hospital, and the day after the suicide of Captain Harvey was discovered. Her body fluids were normal, the chemistry of her system unscrambled, her kidneys working, and her heart once again seemed strong and steady. Terry Jo had survived yet again, but her condition was still precarious. Many severely dehydrated people like her have died after being rescued, their organs too damaged to recover.

She was offered a small portion of eggs for breakfast and an equally small helping of turkey for lunch, and she ate all she was given. On Sunday, November 19, she progressed to a regular diet. She ate, smiled, and acted like any normal child, and Verdon was overjoyed with her progress. Now she was out of the woods physically, with all danger past, but what of her mental condition?

She never mentioned her parents, brother, or sister. She did, however, write her doctor several notes that said: "If I am asleep when you come to see me, PLEASE WAKE ME UP!" She had obviously latched on to him as a source of security – and maybe she didn't want to sleep because of her fears of whatever demons might inhabit her dreams.

She had other worries, too, that would occupy her mind as she lay in her hospital bed: How would she pay for all of this care now that she was all alone? How would she get back home to Green Bay all by herself? (She worried about this even though her aunt and uncle had rushed to Miami from Wisconsin.) Where would she live with no family? How would she buy food and clothes? All this worrying – but Terry Jo was anything but alone and had been embraced by so many, including medical staff deeply touched by her plight and moved by her grit, who would never dream of asking for payment. Many of the medical staff, most especially Dr. Verdon, put in long hours caring for the little girl from the raft. One sign of how the story of the sea waif who had lost her family moved the entire country was the letters that arrived, written by dozens of families across the country who offered to adopt her. One of those offers came from the very same remarkable man who was treating her. Dr. Verdon and his wife already had seven children. Clearly, the attachment Terry Jo felt for him was reciprocated.

Terry Jo's worries were evidence of just how lost and abandoned she felt. She put up the bravest of fronts, however.

One other thought occupied Terry Jo's mind, and would for a long time to come: Where was her father? She had not seen or heard him that night, and he was the only member of her family she could not account for. (She had been told that her sister's body had been found.) Maybe he, too, had jumped overboard and had miraculously made it to one of the many Bahama islands and was waiting to be found. Terry Jo, it would later be revealed, had seen her mother, and brother, dead and she had accepted that. She had not seen her father – and she needed him.

Verdon was not concerned that she wasn't talking about what she had been through. "I don't want her to re-live what happened until she is ready, until she decides for herself," he said. "I'll let her take her own good time."

Her room was closely guarded, even after she was on the mend, though from what, no one had any idea. Up to now, no one had been admitted except the doctors; a private nurse; Terry Jo's uncle – her father's brother, Fred Duperrault of Milwaukee – and her Aunt Dotty – Mrs. Ralph Scheer, who was her father's sister from Green Bay. Reporters were not allowed to talk to her.

Dr. Verdon finally notified Coast Guard investigators that Terry Jo would tell her story to them the next day. This was the moment for which everyone waited.

She was propped up on pillows, surrounded by flowers and dolls, when the Coast Guard investigators arrived. Her left arm hugged a huge, blonde doll sent to her by her saviors from the *Captain Theo*. Somehow the crew had gotten wind of the fact that Terry Jo's beloved life-size doll (and her sister's as well) had gone down with the *Bluebelle*. With her right hand, she ran a comb through her bleached hair.

She greeted the officers with a gleaming, and very brave, smile. She was a portrait in innocence and courage. This brought sudden lumps to the throats of the officers when they thought about what this little girl putting up the brave front must have gone through. Little did they know.

The doctor whispered, "Don't be misled by that smile. She doesn't fully realize at this moment what has happened."

In fact, Terry Jo realized a great deal, even if she didn't let on. She was keeping most of her thoughts to herself.

No one had told her yet that she was, barring another miracle, an orphan. But except for holding out hope that her father might somehow have survived, she knew. On the *Captain Theo*, she had pointed thumbs down, an indication that she realized everyone was dead. But, in the hospital, she never brought up the subject, not even to her aunt and uncle, and no one had dared to ask.

At this point, no one had told her that Captain Harvey had survived the sinking. She did not know what he had told the Coast Guard, nor was she aware that he had then killed himself.

The closed-door interrogation was conducted by Captain Barber and Lieutenant Murdock in the privacy of Terry Jo's hospital room, with her doctor and nurse in attendance.

"Terry," Murdock said gently, "Captain Barber is going to ask you a question. Will you reply close to the microphone?" She nodded and smiled. Then, speaking in a low child's voice, but clearly and distinctly, she told how her family had traveled to Florida on a dream vacation, chartered the *Bluebelle*, and embarked on the voyage to the Bahamas.

"Can you tell us if everything went well and if it was a happy trip up until the night of the accident?" Barber asked. He chose the neutral word "accident" deliberately, so as not to influence the nature of her account and not to upset her. (In fact, for many years after, Terry Jo herself always referred to the *Bluebelle* tragedy as "the accident.")

"Yes, everything was OK."

"Now, this is a difficult part to tell us about," Barber continued. "But would you, in your own words, as best as you can, tell us what happened that night on the *Bluebelle*? I know it is difficult."

Terry Jo's story came out, then, in words strong and clear and not disrupted by the emotions that had to be there – a story that everyone had begun to dread ever since the skipper's bloody body had been found on the floor of the motel bathroom.

At about nine o'clock, on the last night of the *Bluebelle*'s existence, Terry Jo had retired below to the small cabin behind the main cabin and gone to sleep alone in its three-quarter berth. Ordinarily, her sister, René, slept there, too, but on this night René remained on deck in the cockpit with all of the others.

Some time during the night, Terry Jo said she was awakened from a peaceful sleep, but not by the howling wind of a squall and the loud crashing of masts and rigging. She was jolted awake instead by a lone, screaming voice from inside the boat that suddenly penetrated her dreams in the quiet, comfortable darkness. It was her brother screaming, "Help, Daddy, help!!" As she heard that chilling scream, she also heard brief running and stamping noises. Then there was silence, except for some vague creaks and normal boat sounds. She lay there shivering, too disoriented and suddenly terrified to go out and see what was happening, and not completely sure that she hadn't just awoken from a nightmare.

After sitting for many minutes (she later estimated five to ten) and hearing no more sounds, she crept, trembling, out of her cabin and saw her mother and brother lying crumpled in the main cabin, a pool of blood collecting on one side of the cabin floor.

Terry Jo had seen death before, but only in the innocent world and innocent way of a child. She had known the death of a grandparent who died in the natural order of things, of a beloved pet dog that she found beside the road where he had been hit by a car, and she had reverently buried the bodies of small animals that she had found in the woods. She knew, too, that another sibling had been stillborn a few years before. But this was far too much for her to absorb in one single, awful moment. Still, she instantly knew that they were dead. And within the shock and confusion and unreality that in one instant consumed her, somehow she still managed to accept the finality of their death right then and there without question. In that same instant, in the fraction of a second it took her to blink her eyes closed and then open again, she left the innocent and safe world of childhood behind – far behind – forever.

In a dreamlike detachment, she watched herself slowly climb the companionway stairs. Fearfully, she poked her head out of the companionway hatch that faced aft into the cockpit. Looking out she saw more blood pooled on the starboard side of the cockpit, and possibly a knife. She stood upright and turned to look toward the front of the boat.

Suddenly Harvey was rushing at her out of the night from the forward part of the deck. She started to say, "What's happening?" but she saw as he got closer his right eye rolling hideously. Already terrified, she found herself in the next instant looking straight into the face of a nightmare, her nightmare. He struck her, shoved her roughly down the stairs and, in a deep, growling voice, commanded her to "Get back down there!"

Her heart pounding, the terrified girl backed down the steps. She returned unsteadily to her cabin, averting her eyes from seeing the awful truth of her mother and brother again. Terry Jo crawled back onto her bunk and huddled, shivering, in the corner, her back against a bulkhead. Her being was so occupied by fear and confusion that she struggled simply to take in what was happening. The mental shock was so great that, even though she knew her mother and brother were dead, she could not marshal her thoughts enough even to begin to wonder about the fates of her father and sister.

She heard water sloshing and she wondered if the captain was washing blood from the deck.

After some more minutes, oily-smelling water from the bilges began to come into her cabin and cover the floor. But still she huddled there in a rigid, shivering silence, afraid to move even though she realized the ship was filling with water.

Suddenly the dark form of the captain was silhouetted in the frame of her doorway. She could only stare, wide-eyed. Where minutes before she had clearly seen the very eye of the face of evil, now she could see only a faceless shadow. He held something in his hands across his body, and stood there for what seemed like ages, looking down at her. He said nothing and the only sounds in the room were his heavy breathing, the thundering of her heart in her ears, and the slap of the rising water against the bulkheads. She held her breath in rigid terror until her lungs ached.

Then the captain simply turned and walked silently out of the cabin, and she heard him climb the companionway stairs back to the upper deck. Next she heard erratic pounding noises from somewhere in the boat.

After an uncertain number of minutes, the oily water began lapping over the top of her mattress.

Terry Jo had no choice but to leave the cabin again and face whatever fate awaited her on the dark unknown of the deck and in the person of the captain, so suddenly sinister and terrifying, who lurked above. Wading through oily, waist-deep water to the companionway stairs in the cabin where the bodies of her brother and mother now floated somewhere, and terrified with the thought that she would bump into a floating body in the dark water, she climbed back up to the top of the steps to the cockpit. There, she raised her head even more fearfully this time, looked around and saw in the illumination from the light at the top of the mizzen that the ship's dinghy and rubber life raft had been launched and were floating beside the boat on the port side.

"Is the ship sinking?" the confused girl cried.

"Yes!" Harvey shouted from behind her toward the front of the boat. He rushed at her again and handed her a line, shouting frantically, "Here! Hold this!" Terry Jo, already numb from shock, stiffened in terror – and the line slipped through her fingers.

Harvey hurried forward. Terry Jo could not see what he went to get. Since the boat was already well down in the water and it was the line to the dinghy that Harvey had hurriedly handed to her, clearly Terry Jo had interrupted him at the very instant he was getting off the *Bluebelle*. When he rushed back seconds later, he cried, "The dinghy's gone!"

The dinghy was now slowly drifting away into the dark from the sinking *Bluebelle*. With no further sound, he dived overboard, abandoning her on a now wave-washed deck. She saw him swimming after the dinghy, but couldn't see if he caught up with it after he disappeared into the night.

Remarkably, the girl from Green Bay who had pretended to be Tarzan and had played fantasy survival games in the woods dug deep and did not panic, and to this clear-headedness she would owe her life. She reported later that for the whole time after she was awakened by her brother's screams, she felt as if she was outside of herself watching her own actions. Such detachment is not unusual in moments of extreme crisis. Yet somehow this young girl had the presence of mind to fight off the horrible unreality of her sudden nightmare, not freeze in panic, and focus on what she had to do: she remembered the five-foot by two-and-one-half-foot white, oblong cork life float that was kept lashed to the right side of the top of the main cabin, which was still just barely above water.

Terry Jo scrambled to the float, over a deck now awash in water. She looked at the knots securing the float and quickly saw how to undo the four half-hitches. Keeping herself calm enough to work with deliberate speed, she carefully pulled the right end of each rope, undid each knot, and worked the float loose. In the very moment she got it free, the deck was falling away from beneath her feet into the dark depths, and the boat's fallen mainsail was billowing on the surface. She had to push the life float, half crawling, half swimming, across the sail and over the cable safety line of the starboard deck rail to get to the open water. She climbed onto the tiny oblong cork, the only thing left that could save her from the depths. Just as she did, a line from the float snagged on the sinking ship. For one breathless moment Terry Jo and the float were both pulled under the water by the plunging *Bluebelle*. But somehow the line came free and Terry Jo popped back up to the surface, into a lonely world of ghostly darkness. She huddled low on the float, rigid with fear that the captain, who only a minute ago was on the other side of the *Bluebelle*, might find her.

Captain Barber brought her thoughts back to her hospital room. "Terry," he said, "when you woke and heard the screams, whose voice did you hear?"

"My brother's."

"Do you have any idea why he screamed?"

"No."

"When you first woke, you heard running and stamping. Do you think it was on the deck overhead?"

She said she thought it was down below in the main cabin right outside her cabin, where she had found the bodies of her mother and Brian lying curled up next to a pool of blood.

"Terry, do you know what Captain Harvey had in his hand when he entered your cabin?"

"I thought it was the rifle," she replied. "We took a rifle [with us on the trip]. I'm not positive, but I think it was the rifle."

As the questioning went on, she remained alert and responsive. Her lips still were swollen and her burned face was greased. Barber, handsome and soft-spoken, turned to more probing questions. But he treated her very gently, moving quickly from one question to another, not allowing her to linger long on the more gruesome parts of her ordeal.

During the *Bluebelle* cruise, before disaster struck, she said she heard no arguments between Captain Harvey and anybody else on board, and she had never seen him angry before that night. As far as she could remember, Harvey had spoken mostly to her father. Terry Jo had hardly talked with him, except to say hello when they were introduced. She did relate, however, that she had seen Harvey's lazy eye one previous time, and that it had given her a momentary chill, but she had soon forgotten about it in the excitement of her family's great adventure. She did not at this time refer to the moment when she had felt oddly uncomfortable, when she had seen Harvey staring at her as she stood in her bathing suit in the shallow water off a Bahamian island.

In reply to other questions, Terry Jo said she had no idea how her mother and Brian got blood on them, and that she saw nothing like a club or other weapon lying near them.

After seeing her mother and brother lying in the main cabin, Terry Jo was immediately certain that they were dead and she had gone right up to the companionway to the upper deck. When she saw the captain, he was coming at her from the forward part of the ship with what she thought was a pail in his hand.

"Did you ask him what he was doing or what happened to your mother and brother?" Barber asked.

"No, I just said, 'What happened?' And he said, 'Get down there'!"

"When he said that, did he seem to be angry or excited?"

"He sounded real mad."

She saw no one on the deck but the captain, Terry Jo said. She did not see her father, sister, or Mrs. Harvey. It was pitch black out over the sea but the deck was lighted, and she remembered that there was no one at the wheel at the rear of the cockpit steering the boat. A moist wind rustled the shrouds, but it was not strong and the *Bluebelle* rode the swells smoothly.

"Why do you think the captain was angry?"

"I thought maybe there was something up forward that he didn't want me to see. He hit me and shoved me down with his hand." (The forward part of the boat was where the hatch that led to the Harveys' forward cabin was located. In retrospect, Harvey might have been hiding any or all of three things: What had happened to his wife, what had happened to Terry Jo's father, and how little René had died.)

"When you went back to your bunk, about how long did you lie there?"

"I think it was about fifteen minutes."

"And you lay there listening. You were frightened and you lay there?"

"Yes."

"Did you hear anything unusual going on during that fifteen minutes?"

"No."

Now Barber turned to a key point of Captain Harvey's story, his recital of a sudden squall and how the main mast had broken inexplicably, plunging down through the deck and hull, and bringing the mizzenmast down in a tangle of rigging onto the deck and the cockpit. He asked Terry Jo if she saw a broken mast or fallen sails.

"The main sail was all wrinkled and going all over, and the mast was leaning," she said. "I wasn't sure if the mizzen was up, but I think it was."

"You mean that the masts were up but the sails were all slack, is that correct?"

"The masts were up, yes."

"You didn't see any damage or broken part on the mast, did you?"

"No."

"Now, most sailing boats lie over at an angle when the sails are up [and wind is filling the sails]. Do you think the mast was lying over further than it should have been?"

Lieutenant Murdock speculated many years later that Harvey might have cut the shrouds on one side of the boat holding the masts firmly upright as part of a quickly abandoned scheme to make it appear that the *Bluebelle* had, in fact, been severely damaged by a storm. This would have caused the masts to be actually leaning and not just appear to be, especially if the boom was way out and pulling the mast over, as Terry Jo seemed to indicate. In addition, it is clear that Harvey must have lowered the mainsail hurriedly without bothering to stow it properly. This is why it was "going all over," according to Terry Jo. The only reason for doing this is that he needed to quickly make the ship lie dead in the water in order to put the dinghy and life raft over the side. And if one is scuttling a boat, there is no reason to stow the sails.

"You've been sailing before, haven't you, Terry?"

"This was the first time."

Actually, it was only the first time she had been on a sailing cruise, not the first time she had been on some kind of sailboat.

"You had been on board the *Bluebelle* several days when this happened?"

"Yes."

"And you know that when you are sailing, the wind holds the sails firm and not fluttering. Do you understand that?"

"Yes."

"Now, you say when you first came up on deck that night the

sails were loose and fluttering?"

"Yes."

"And did you mean that the main sail was part-way down or just it was loose and fluttering?"

"It was part-way down."

"Terry," Barber said, "did you see anything on the deck that looked like there had been trouble?"

"I saw blood."

"Where did you see the blood?"

"On the deck near the cockpit."

"Did you notice anything lying around there like a club or anything that might have been used as a club?"

"No."

"Did you at any time hear something that might have been a shot?"

"No."

"You say you saw nobody on deck except the captain, but you saw the blood. Could you have seen others if they had been there?"

"I suppose I could, because there was a lot of light. It was coming from lights on top of the sail."

Since she could see the entire cabin top, the deck on either side of the cabin top, and much of the foredeck beyond the cabin top from a standing position in the companionway, this suggests that if Harvey had also killed Dr. Duperrault and Mrs. Harvey, they were either already overboard, or had been put below in the forward cabin. There was no other place they could possibly be. It would make sense for Harvey to put them in the forward cabin if he wanted to cover a crime; i.e., not risk bodies with severe wounds on them possibly being found floating in the sea. The fact that there was blood in the cockpit leaves little doubt that there had been a murderous assault topside as well as below decks. The puzzle: where was René? If she was dead already, how did she die and where was her body? If she was still alive, where was she? Why did Terry Jo neither see nor hear her, either below decks or topside?

"This light, this is the one that is always lighted up on the mast when the boat is sailing at night. Is that the one?"

"Yes."

The light that the lieutenant referred to is a masthead light designed to make the boat visible to other boats at night. Such a light is not designed to direct a lot of light down toward the deck. It is possible, therefore, that there was also a small floodlight attached near the top of the mast that pointed down toward the deck. Otherwise, there could not have been "a lot of light." Many other boats like the *Bluebelle* would have had a pair of floodlights under the spreader that separates and tensions the shrouds high up on the mainmast to illuminate the deck at night. Also, it is clear that regardless of where the lights were located, if light was illuminating the deck from high on a mast, obviously the masts were intact.

Captain Barber asked if she had seen a fire or evidence of fire on the boat. No, she said, but there was a strong odor like that of oil.

"But you did not see any fire at any time, is that correct?"

"That's correct."

"And you did not smell any smoke? You recognize the smell of smoke and fire, don't you? You did not smell anything like a fire?"

"No."

In reply to more questions, she told in greater detail of her second trip to the deck, of struggling with the life-float lashings, and of drifting away from the *Bluebelle*, not knowing if Harvey was out there in the dinghy in the direction she was being pushed by the waves. As she floated away in the quiet darkness, a brief shower passed over and large drops sparked phosphorescent flashes on the surface of the dark water.

Terry Jo was getting tired and jittery. Dr. Verdon interrupted the interrogation and examined her. He indicated that the stress of the interview was causing her heart to beat erratically again and that she needed to rest quietly. She was still not out of the woods. He motioned to the investigators and they withdrew.

Terry Jo's story hit the second floor of Mercy Hospital like a hammer. It soon hit Miami and Green Bay and the country just as hard.

Harvey had lied. There had been no accident.

He had been no mere coward; there had most likely been murder committed aboard the *Bluebelle*.

CHAPTER EIGHT

Eternal Father

"Eternal Father, strong to save,
Whose arm hath bound the restless wave,
Who bidd'st the mighty ocean deep,
Its own appointed limits keep;
Oh, hear us when we cry to Thee,
For those in peril on the sea!"

Eternal Father, Strong to Save (The Navy Hymn)

No one knew at the time she was found how the "sea waif" came to be alone on the sea, and she would be in no condition to tell anyone for some days. Perhaps she had survived a disaster just as Harvey had described it and simply had floated away in the darkness, thanks to finding one of the floats Harvey himself said he had tossed overboard.

As daunting as all of the unanswered questions were, imagining what Terry Jo had gone through in four days without food and water alone on the sea, broiling by day and then freezing by night, was even worse. Less than an hour before she came to be adrift on the float, she had been snug in her berth on her family's too-good-to-be-true sailing cruise, as secure as any child anywhere who sleeps soundly surrounded by her loving family in a very peaceful place

– and who sleeps knowing also that her family is, in turn, being shepherded by a brave war hero.

Then the sudden unreality of death and horror and terror and a sinking ship, and the stunned and terrified child finds herself suddenly and utterly alone on the vast sea, supported by a puny oblong ring of cork and its frayed rope webbing. In an instant, her world has shrunk from the large encompassing security of the majestic and maternal *Bluebelle* that had embraced her family, to a few square feet of rope mesh bordered by canvas-wrapped cork.

Paradoxically, her world has also expanded to the vast open sea on which she drifts and the endless open sky above her. She escaped a sudden death at the hands of the captain, and a slow death by drowning trapped below decks in a sinking boat, only to be vulnerable now to a slower death from dehydration, or to the horror of jaws striking from the dark depths. And no one in the universe knew she was there.

In fact, Terry Jo was alone twice over; she was not only a solitary vulnerable speck on the ocean, she was an orphan. Unless her father and sister had somehow managed to escape and survive, she had no family.

Terry Jo had no water, no food, no cover against the penetrating cold of the night or the blazing heat and scorching sun of the day. She was at the mercy of the indifferent sea. The pale quarter moon had set and heavy clouds scudding across the skies denied her even the small friendly light of the stars. She was all alone in a black void in which she could hear and feel but could not see. And, too, she knew that the terrifying Captain Harvey with his wild eye was out there, somewhere. She spent much of the night

ALONE

scrunched down and still, trying to hide from him. And she talked to God and asked for his protection. At first she didn't even look up for fear that she might see something. All the while, the wind moaned in her ears like a ghost floating with her in the night.

Now the sea of the Bahamas was no longer a thing of joy and beauty, as it had been during the idyllic first days of the voyage. It was vast, foreboding, and dark. Waves built up unseen and broke without warning over her tiny float, and she rubbed stinging salt water out of her eyes and licked the salt from her lips. A sudden tropical shower drenched her and she began to shiver uncontrollably, but some salt was washed from her face and lips and she managed to lick a few drops of brackish water.

She had nothing to protect her from the chill of the night but a thin, white blouse and pink pedal pushers of light, tropical-weight cloth. Perhaps it was a blessing that she was in a state of shock from that night from hell, numbing her to some of the new terrors she faced.

All through the night she huddled, fighting to cling to her life raft as it rose and fell on the swells of the sea. The webbed rope bottom of the float was two or three inches under the surface, so Terry Jo was always sitting in the water. But the water felt good on her skin at first because it was warmer than the chilling wind. She was afraid to move at all, stiff with fear and cold and shock. She tried to draw some small feeling of security from the webbing that held her away from the grasping, dark waters below, and from the thin rim of canvas-covered cork that was all that stood between her and the vast empty sea around her, and the captain with the wild eye. One thought began to occupy her: Where is my father? Maybe he got away somehow, too. Wishing for her father to be OK gradually became a prayer, and she began to talk to God and to ask His protection for her, her father, and her sister.

Sometime later during the night, the skies cleared and she finally raised her head to see a great bowl of millions of bright stars overhead. They increased her feeling of the unreal vastness of this world of water and sky. She felt like she was in some kind of strange, cosmic dream, drifting alone through a dark infinity with nothing to hold onto but herself. She continued to talk to God, and to wrestle with confusion about what had happened. The small raft rose and fell, sailing on and on, carrying its little passenger. It seemed an eternity before the first weak light of dawn broke over the sea.

A flood of light from the rising sun Monday morning dispelled some of the demons of the night, and her mind cleared somewhat. It was easier to feel real in the light, much as it was hard not to feel unreal in the vast dreamlike dark. But, if possible, the light made her more conscious of how alone and vulnerable she was. All of her senses told her so. But as she looked around, there was no sign of Captain Harvey. Feeling safer, a lot of her fear dissipated and, as vulnerable as she was, she said she never felt that afraid again. However, she did say that she continued to fear putting her feet in the water lest she would feel something bump them. Undoubtedly, her fear was blunted by the numbing effects of shock; but compared to the nightmare horrors of the *Bluebelle* and the terrors and unreality of her first night adrift, her situation had – as strange as it is to say it – improved.

All around her she could see nothing but a wasteland of water. She could only see a short distance because she was so close to the sea. Even when she sat up on the ring of the float, with her feet dangling in the water, her horizons were close. But when she did sit up, she found that the float was so light that it threatened to tip over if her weight was mostly on one side of it. It was not designed to be sat in, but rather held onto by people in the water.

The morning sun's warm rays felt good at first as they drove the chill from her slender body. But soon she realized that the sun brought her new and greater danger. As the day wore on, its heat became oppressive. On the shadeless sea, the air temperature quickly rose to 85 degrees. The scorching sun on her unprotected skin was much hotter. She found some relief from the heat by submerging as much of her body as possible in the water in the net, but as she did, one of the pieces of webbing broke. More would break as the days wore on.

Unfortunately, the break exposed her even more to the sharp beaks of two parrot fish that had begun to peck away at her buttocks and legs, giving her starts of fear. They would stay with her constantly. Eventually she would get angry at them rather than afraid, showing her feisty side; she took a few angry swats at them, but she had the sense not to flail and make a commotion that could draw the attention of far more dangerous creatures from the deep. They certainly could see her from below silhouetted against the light of the sky. Interestingly, though, she did not feel much fear of creatures that might grab her from the deep, even though that might be everyone else's nightmare.

The sunlight glaring off the salty surface of the sea was murderous and the salt on her skin hastened the burning, much as the salt on her lips aggravated her thirst. Her light clothing offered her little protection, and she had no hat to cover her head, only a healthy mass of blonde hair, and it seemed that her brain was cooking. Her salty skin crawled and tightened painfully under the intense sun, and her face stung as the dry, burning skin drew taut.

By mid-afternoon of the first day, body fluids were evaporating through her skin and with every breath. Exposure, dehydration, and heat exhaustion would soon begin to scramble her body chemistry.

Far above, fleecy white clouds moved with the trade winds, but there was no rain in them. Even though she had not eaten and was becoming dehydrated, she felt no great hunger or thirst. This is true even though her tongue was becoming dry, her saliva thick, and her throat parched. Her body temperature was rising. The absence of both great fear, and hunger and thirst strongly suggest that Terry Jo remained in a strong state of shock. In a day or two she would be unconscious. In three this abandoned child would be dead, if she didn't fall off the raft and drown before then. Or be taken by sharks.

She had nothing but her own young and healthy body and grit to help her fight for her life. There was food in the sea around her, but she had no way to get it – except for clumps of Sargasso that floated by. She saw brown berries in the clumps and thought about eating them, but the idea of eating something salty did not appeal to her, so she didn't. She needed water more desperately with each blistering hour. She did see a ship in the distance that afternoon of the first day, but it was too far away to notice her. She would see others pass her by, too.

As the sun set, she briefly felt neither too hot nor too cold.

But as the light began to fade, she felt again both the rising cold and the dread of the night. But she did fall asleep that Monday night. She dreamed of diving and swimming back home, only to awaken in sudden cold, choking panic to realize that she was in the sea. She had fallen off the life float. Fortunately, her left arm was still draped over the edge of the float, and she was able to pull herself back into the light and tippy craft. After she got back onto the float, trembling with fear, another piece of the webbing in the bottom broke.

As she balanced herself across the edges of the float to take her weight off the webbing, she saw the light of a lighthouse, probably the one at Great Stirrup Cay, only eight or so miles southwest of where she would have been at that time in the Providence Channel – and where there would have been a snug anchorage for the *Bluebelle* and her family the night before. Strangely, she found that her sudden dip and its adrenaline surge had refreshed and reinvigorated her.

Later that night – or perhaps it was the following night – she thought she heard waves crashing on rocks. It is extremely unlikely that she had drifted near enough to an island for this to have been true, considering that she was being pushed by a breeze from the southeast and a current heading west. More probably it was a hallucination or a dream.

Several times during the second day planes flew overhead and she waved her arms. Most of them were high and flew straight. But one small, red plane in particular flew a back-and-forth grid pattern above her. Then it circled overhead. She watched it for a long time and waved at it, even removing and waving her blouse. At one point it dived down in her direction as if coming closer to investigate something. She waved frantically, her heart pounding with hope. But the plane passed directly over her, close enough that she could see the details of its underside, but at just the wrong angle for the pilots to look down and spot her. The plane climbed away and flew off. Terry Jo was crushed.

She didn't know that that very plane was searching for possible survivors of the *Bluebelle*. A search had been mounted that afternoon, right after Harvey had been picked up by the *Gulf Lion*. It included two aircraft and two Coast Guard cutters, plus alerts had been sent to ships in the area to be on the lookout. The official search area covered some 5,000 square miles of the Northwest Providence Channel between Grand Bahama Island to the north, Great Stirrup Cay to the south, Great Abaco Island to the east, and the Gulf Stream to the west. The problem for Terry Jo was that even from a plane at low altitude, her small white float (plus her blonde hair, white blouse, and pale pants) would have looked like just another little whitecap among millions of whitecaps tumbling over the blue surface of the sea. The only way she would have been spotted was if a plane had flown low and close enough for a pilot to see her by looking off to the side. And the only way a Coast Guard cutter would find her was if it happened to come very close. No ship had.

Commercial planes flying from Florida to the Bahamas and back, and smaller aircraft plying the islands came and went. Each time engines faded in the distance, her spirits dropped a little lower, and again the only sounds around her were the slapping, grumbling noises of the waves.

She was floating in the Northwest Providence Channel, a deep spot in a predominately shallow region. The channel is, in fact, the northernmost reach of an unusually deep trench called the Tongue of the Ocean. The seven hundred low-lying islands and cays of the Bahamas, stretching from near the Florida coast to a point just over the horizon from Haiti, are the exposed peaks of a great submarine mountain range. Terry Jo was drifting over a mile-deep canyon between mountains.

In the shallow areas of the Bahamas, seas are gentle in the wintertime, but here in the deeps the waters grow mean in a moderate wind. A fifteen-knot wind out of the east pushed up swells eight feet tall, almost twice the height of the little rider on the inches-high raft.

Prevailing winds affect the current of the channel, but the winds generally push toward the west-northwest in the same direction as the current, and gradually she was drifting in that direction. Terry Jo was moving inexorably to join the mighty Gulf Stream. If she was not rescued, her raft would drift on and on, first north with the Gulf Stream and then east, carrying her body in a great sweeping arc across the wide Atlantic to the British Isles, unless it was overturned by some angry wave, to drop her into the depths with the other ghosts of the *Bluebelle*.

Fortunately, the second day on the float dawned cloudy and cooler. Several ships passed during the day, for the Providence Channel was a major shipping lane. Some seemed very distant, others closer. She even tried paddling toward a couple of them, but she had the sense after awhile not to waste too much energy or to draw attention to her. The nearest island of Great Stirrup Cay was only a few miles south of her raft, but it might as well have been a thousand. The way she was headed, there was no chance that the southeasterly winds and the westward current would carry her to some friendly beach – unless the winds veered southerly or, even better, came from the southwest. That might have been enough to counteract the effects of the westward current and to deposit her on the long southern shore of Grand Bahama Island to her north. (That same shore was where later Lieutenant Murdock and Captain Barber would walk for days, looking for debris from the *Bluebelle*. None was ever found. This is likely because any debris would have drifted only slightly north of west, like Terry Jo, on a path that led to the Gulf Stream, and then north.)

Terry Jo knew too well that sharks prowled the deep beneath her. Indeed, a couple of days earlier she had watched her brother, Brian, catch a barracuda, and she had seen the fin of a shark from the security of the *Bluebelle*. Yet, while floating, she remained mostly unafraid. Once, her raft drifted into a massive school of small fish that darkened the sea all around her. Sharks undoubtedly followed these schools, scooping them up in their great mouths. Fortunately for Terry Jo, the sharks must have been small ones – or well-fed. Barracuda were also there, and she had heard that they strike at colored objects. She worried that her pink pedal pushers might attract them through the web bottom of the float.

In fact, Terry Jo might have been protected in a surprising way: the waist-deep water she had waded through in the cabin of the *Bluebelle* had been covered by a film of oil and gasoline, and because the boat was sinking slowly in calm seas, she had launched the float into an oil slick that would inevitably have formed around the boat in those conditions. The slight coating of oil on the float (and especially soaked up by the rope webbing and her clothing) might have been just enough to mask her odor from predators.

A flock of sea gulls, drawn by the commotion, appeared overhead and dived for scraps of fish left by the barracuda. Several hovered over the raft, suspended in the wind, staring curiously at its little passenger. The birds gave Terry Jo a burst of hope that an island might be within paddling distance. But when she sat as upright as far as she safely could, she could see nothing. One gull came down for a closer look and seemed about to alight on the ring of the float, but Terry Jo moved and, with an excited flapping of wings, it was gone.

Just as it flew away, Terry Jo saw some large, dark shapes just breaking the surface some yards from her raft. Her heart caught in her throat. They came closer and she thought they might be porpoises, but they were too large and dark and had great bulbous heads. They swam placidly near her, some twenty to thirty feet away, staring at her with large, impassive, dark eyes that barely broke above the surface of the water, spouting regularly as they breathed. The great whooshing sounds of their breaths spoke to Terry Jo and seemed to say, "We are life. You are not alone. We are here with you." Terry Jo was immensely comforted by the presence of these gentle giants. She said a little prayer of thanks to God for sending them. They remained nearby for hours.

Experts later decided that Terry Jo was kept company for a time by a pod of pilot whales, a species of large dolphin that grow to about twenty feet in length – and which are predators, though they tend to hunt squid.

As the piercing sun broke through the clouds in the after-noon, Terry Jo splashed some water over her suddenly hot, drawn skin. How far away were the cool forests of Wisconsin and the cold waters of Green Bay? She had water-skied on the bay but she wasn't very good at it, and had taken many a tumble into the cold water. Not pleasant at the time, it was now something she desperately wished for, especially because the waters of Lake Michigan were fresh, not saline.

The sun dropped and finally sank below the horizon. Tuesday night came on and brought back the awful unknown of the dark, but it also brought blessed relief to her scorched body. Briefly she traded physical relief for increased psychological torment – until she began, again, to shiver from the cold as well as the mind-bending dark. Her temperature fell but she continued to suffer from heat exhaustion. Of the forty pounds of fluid in her body, she probably had lost five during the day. Her mouth was almost unbearably dry and she could muster no saliva. It was difficult to swallow.

Through that cold third night, her raft rose and fell, gradually pitching on toward the west-northwest, and she somehow fell into a deep sleep. That night she had some hallucinatory dreams full of vivid images: oddly, although she had never flown, she dreamed that she was in the cockpit of an airliner coming in for a landing, and she saw the long, straight, converging lines of iridescent landing lights standing out with surreal brilliance against a deep, shiny blackness. Despite never having been in an airplane, the image she saw was exactly as it would look from a cockpit coming in for a night landing. The psychedelic nature of this dream indicates how the combination of trauma, exhaustion, isolation, and dehydration were beginning to bend her mind.

She also saw her father, seated peacefully and drinking a

glass of red wine. Although she had never tasted wine, it looked extremely refreshing; just what she needed to quench her thirst. And she heard his voice call out to her: "Come on Terry Jo! We're leaving now!"

Occasionally, a wave splashing into her face brought her into semi-consciousness. She was so numb now from shock, she felt even less fear. The confined world of the raft and the water was beginning to become her way of life. The previous world of the *Bluebelle*, her family, and her home was becoming strangely distant and incomprehensible.

Wednesday dawned bright and clear, and it grew hot very quickly. The glare of the sun caused her dry, scratchy, and dimming eyes severe pain. She was now beyond hunger. More moisture was sapped from her body. All her muscles ached. Her skin burned through her blouse and pedal pushers. Her lips were rough and swollen. She had to balance rigidly on the edges of the unsteady float more and more because so much of the rope webbing had broken away. She hallucinated more now, even seeing the classic image of the tiny desert island complete with a solitary palm tree. She tried paddling toward it, but it disappeared. She slowly became delirious and, finally, lapsed into unconsciousness. That she managed to stay on the float in that condition is remarkable.

Was she back in the arms of her mother? Back in the safety of home, freed of her memories of the awful sea and the dark, bloody night on the *Bluebelle*?

The seas grew rougher and tossed her raft, but she didn't notice it. During the afternoon, she became comatose, her body shuddered in what might have been mild convulsions, but she was not aware of it. If her will to live had been weak, she might have died that day. The east wind was up to twenty knots and the taller waves towered thirteen feet over the raft. Somehow, she did not fall from the raft.

In the cold of yet another night, her temperature again dropped and only for brief periods was she close to being awake and rational. But she also had dreams of landing on an island and finding her father. With every moment of semi-consciousness came renewed suffering. Lack of water had slowed her circulation and less and less blood was flowing to her heart as it thickened from severe dehydration. Her whole body was afire and her legs were racked by cramps from the loss of critical electrolytes and from the awkward positions she had to maintain to stay balanced on the float.

She had found, after much experimentation, that the best and most stable way to sit in the lightweight raft was across the width of it with her shoulders resting on one edge, her arms stretched out on either side along the rim, her bottom on the webbing (and in the water), and her thighs up on the other edge with her feet out of the water. This position kept much of her weight on the edges of the float and off the fragile webbing.

Generally she felt less and less, and had less sense of where she was. All hunger had long since left her. Without water, she no longer had saliva, and her body was saving all of its remaining fluids for her vital organs, so she had no digestive juices. If she had had food, she couldn't have eaten it.

She didn't so much sleep that fourth night as drift in and out of consciousness. Though just as cold as the previous nights, she did not feel it.

ALONE

When the cruel sun rose Thursday, she did not feel its burning rays either. She was in the deep sleep that drifts close to the threshold of death. Her reflexes were almost gone and her blood pressure was falling fast. Her temperature had risen close to a dangerous 105 degrees. But somehow she still kept her precarious balance on the pitiful piece of cork.

The sea was rough at first in the morning. Walls of steep, tumbling water, green mountains capped with white spume pushed by a stiff breeze, came at her in formation, one after another. Her raft was lifted high up on the tops of steep cliffs, then lowered into dark valleys. It was a miracle that it did not capsize and throw her body out to be swallowed up by the hungry ocean. As she lay unconscious, her body still in the shape of a crucifix with arms extended along the float rim, her hands were locked on the rim in a painful death grip. The waves broke over her constantly. But the cooling water may have prolonged her life just a little bit longer.

Only the faintest spark now flickered in her sore and tortured body. Severely dehydrated, her fluids were going mostly to her heart and lungs, and less to her brain, which was shutting down. Her kidneys had stopped working. Yet, in midmorning, she somehow rallied out of her deep stupor and opened her dry, sore, and barely focusing eyes.

Through her stupor she had sensed something. And, through the mist of half-consciousness and dim eyes, a huge, shadowy shape loomed before her like some great, rumbling, dark beast. Its rumble was so deep that she could feel its pounding rhythm in her chest. As she watched, it seemed to metamorphose from an unworldly vessel floating above the sea to a great whale, and then into a solid black wall suspended in the air above her. When she looked up to the top of that great wall, she saw heads and waving arms. She could dimly make out voices shouting. She sensed that they were telling her to stay put.

Digging deeper than she ever had in her life, with a supreme effort she struggled into a half-sitting position. She lifted an arm and managed a feeble wave, then toppled back onto the float. Somewhere, she found the strength to pull herself upright again and make a piteous effort to paddle with her hands. Her fiery will to survive still lived. Then she looked up and saw that barrels were being lowered over the side of the great chugging machine and figures were moving them together in the water. She fell back again, too spent to hold herself up anymore. Finally the strong arms of strange, powerful beings speaking an alien tongue were picking her up, and she felt herself suspended limply in space, being lifted slowly up and up as she slid back into oblivion.

Sailors aboard the Greek freighter Captain Theo *gather around Terry Jo's blanketed form shortly after her rescue from the waters of the Northwest Providence Channel.*

CHAPTER NINE

Recovering

Terry Jo's hospital room was closely guarded against the frenzy surrounding the fate of the *Bluebelle* and against the uncertainty created by the suicide of the captain. Here, she played – seemingly happily – with dolls, stuffed dogs, games, and many other presents sent to her by a sympathetic public. Her story had stirred wonder, sympathy, and admiration around the world.

By Thanksgiving Day, November 23, she was able to order a turkey dinner with all the fixings. She had only her aunt and uncle from Green Bay with her on a day when close-knit families traditionally gathered, but she seemed cheerful and was smiling and she ate heartily. Terry Jo still had given no indication that she was aware of her family's fate. She had not cried and she had asked no questions. People read the lack of tears as a sign of bravery, and they were partly right. In fact, for the next several years she would hear herself referred to as "brave little Terry Jo." There was little doubt that she knew her family was gone although it would be years before she would come to accept that her father, whom she never saw that terrible night and whose body was never found, had died with everyone else.

Her sunburned skin was peeling but her physical recovery now was complete. Dr. Verdon examined her and said she would soon be ready for release from the hospital. She had snapped back with amazing vitality from her agonizing ordeal on the raft.

Four days later, on November 27, eager to close any gaps in Terry Jo's story of the *Bluebelle* disaster, Coast Guard investigators called on her again.

Captain Barber showed her a sketch of the *Bluebelle* deck. "This," he said, "is what the vessel might have looked like that night if things happened as people said they happened. Now, Mr. Harvey told us that a large part of the main mast broke off and fell down through the deck and bottom of the boat. Now, if this happened the way he said, the cable, the rigging, the sails, the mizzenmast would have been lying all over the deck, a terrific bundle of wires and sail, a real mess. Now, can you remember if you saw any such mess as that all over the deck?"

She shook her head firmly. "There wasn't any mess at all," she said.

Barber: "You told us that when you went up on deck that first time, that there was light on the deck, from the light up near the sails or on the mast. Do you remember saying that?"

Terry Jo: "Yes."

Barber: "And you have a clear recollection of this light, and the masts were standing up?"

Terry Jo: "Yes."

Barber: "This point is quite important because Mr. Harvey's story is all based on the fact that these masts came falling down. You told us the last time that one of the masts was tipping over, slanted over a little bit. Can you tell us again what you thought you saw?"

Terry Jo: "I had thought that maybe something hit it and it

was laying over that way."

Barber: "Do you understand that this mast is normally straight up on the deck?"

Terry Jo: "Yes."

Barber: "And you feel, looking back, that one or both were leaning? Can you describe why you believe this?"

Terry Jo: "Because when I put the raft over the side, the boom was way out and the sail was kind of out in the water and the mast was leaning that way." She held up a fountain pen indicating that the mast was leaning about ten degrees from vertical. Of course, by the time she was up on deck and launching the raft, it is entirely possible that the boat, filled with water, was listing to the side where the boom was way out. That could have made it appear that the mast was leaning.

Barber: "Terry, when you first went up on deck, did you notice any damage to the rigging wire, the stays holding the masts up?"

Terry Jo: "All the wires were perfect."

Barber: "Mr. Harvey told us that when the main mast fell down, this dragged over the mizzen mast. The rigging between dragged over the mizzenmast, which fell down and struck the deck. Did you notice the mizzenmast down on the deck?"

Terry Jo: "It was standing up."

Barber: "Terry, in looking back now, do you believe that Mr. Harvey harmed any of your family?"

Terry Jo hesitated. "I really don't know, because – he might have."

Barber: "Do you remember any arguments between Mr.

Harvey and anybody on the boat?"

Terry Jo: "No."

Barber: "As best you can remember, he was not angry with anybody on the boat?"

Terry Jo: "No."

Replying to more questions, Terry Jo said she and René ordinarily slept together on the three-quarter berth in the small aft sleeping cabin, but on the night of the disaster, she had gone to bed by herself. Her father had planned to stay on top during the night and help Captain Harvey with the steering, and René was to come down later to sleep with her mother in the main cabin. Mrs. Harvey sometimes stayed on deck all night, too.

Barber: "Mr. Harvey told us that all of you were on deck when the mishap happened, that you were asleep in your mother's lap in the cockpit at the time. Was that a true statement?"

Terry Jo: "No."

Barber: "Was it absolutely wrong?"

Terry Jo: "Yes."

She said she didn't know if René ever came below that night.

Barber: "Terry, when you first woke up that night and came out of the cabin, I believe you told us you saw your mother and brother lying on the floor. Did you go close to them?"

Terry Jo: "No, but when I looked they were both lying on their backs close together in front of the kitchen door. I couldn't tell what caused the blood."

Barber: "When you first went up on deck, you told us that you saw Mr. Harvey with something in his hand which could have been a pail or bucket. Did you get the impression that he did not want you to come forward toward the forecastle?"

Terry Jo: "Yes."

Barber: "Please tell us why you had that impression."

Terry Jo: "I thought there was a whole bunch of blood and stuff and he thought that would make me sick, so he made me go below."

Barber: "Terry, I believe you know now that Mr. Harvey did away with himself after he learned that you were alive. Do you know why he did that?"

Terry Jo: "No."

Barber: "When you first were awakened that night by screaming sounds and stamping of feet, you told us that you heard your brother scream. Did you hear anything else?"

Terry Jo: "No, but my brother was saying, 'Help, Daddy, Help!'"

Barber: "You heard this quite clearly?"

Terry Jo: "Yes."

Barber: "You didn't hear anyone else say anything?"

Terry Jo: "No."

Barber: "Did you ever find out what the stamping noise was?"

Terry Jo: "I thought it was my brother stamping."

Barber: "By that, you mean you're not sure whether the noise came from the upper deck or the lower deck [the main cabin]?"

Terry Jo: "I think it was the lower deck. I wasn't sure."

When the screams stopped, she said, she heard someone pound up the companionway stairs.

Barber: "Then, when you went up on deck and saw Mr. Harvey come toward you, how did he look?"

Terry Jo: "He seemed angry."

Barber: "Did you notice any blood or cuts or bruises on him?"

Terry Jo: "No."

Barber: "Later, when the captain came into your room, do you still believe he had a rifle in his hand?"

Terry Jo: "Yes."

Barber: "When you were first awakened, how long did you lie in your bunk before you got up?"

Terry Jo: "It might have been five minutes or ten minutes."

Barber: "Was the door to your room closed?"

Terry Jo: "Yes."

Barber: "Before you got up, you thought you heard someone going up the stairs. Is that right?"

Terry Jo: "Yes."

Barber: "Do you think that your mother and brother were in such a position that they could have fallen down those stairs?"

Terry Jo: "I don't think they fell down."

Barber: "How long was it from the time you first awakened until you left the vessel in the life float?"

Terry Jo: "About a half hour."

Barber: "How deep was the water in your room when you got up the last time?"

Terry Jo: "Up to my waist."

Barber: "Terry, Mr. Harvey told us that after the mast fell down and he went forward to get the cable cutters, he could not get back to the stern because a fire broke out between him and the others. Will you tell us again if you saw or smelled or in any way detected a fire that night?"

Terry Jo: "I was positive there wasn't any fire, but I did smell something like oil or something from the engine because the engine was right down near my room."

(The engine room was in the middle of the rear of the boat, right next to her cabin. If the engine room was flooding with water, a smell of oil would be virtually inevitable, as oily water is always present in the bilge, or very bottom, of a boat with an internal engine.)

Barber: "Had you ever been in your room [cabin] when the main engine was running?"

Terry Jo: "Yes. It was running that night. When I went up the first time and came down again the engine started." She said this was when she began to smell oil and noticed the water starting to rise in her room.

The sea was not rough, Terry Jo said, and the vessel was not listing much at the time.

Barber: "When you got to the life float just before the vessel went down, were there any sails or rigging in your way that you had to climb over or worm through? Any sails or anything of that type?"

Terry Jo: "Well, the boom was down in the water and the sail was there, too, and when I put the life raft out, it was on the sail."

Barber: "But there was no rigging or wires in your way?"

Terry Jo: "No."

Barber: "That night before you went down to bed, was there any rain?"

Terry Jo: "No, but as soon as I got off on the raft it started to rain."

Barber: "Did you see the *Bluebelle* go down?"

Terry Jo: "No."

It would have been impossible to see the *Bluebelle* go down in the pitch dark night, once the lights were extinguished.

The questions continued.

"How long did it take the *Bluebelle* to sink after you left?" Murdock asked.

"As soon as I got off. I didn't look back."

The second interrogation left the Coast Guard even more convinced of the truth of Terry Jo's story and firm in their belief that Harvey had killed the others aboard the *Bluebelle*.

"We have no reason whatever to doubt her," Murdock said.

"There was no wreckage when she ran up to the deck – wreckage that would have had to be there if Harvey's story were true.

"Her story is more convincing than ever. This child could not possibly be evading anything. We asked her the questions in the roughest sort of way. We planned the questions with the idea of trying to trip her up. She told a straightforward story and did not deviate from it."

Barber said he didn't believe it had really occurred to Terry Jo yet that Harvey might have murdered those aboard. Indeed, for years afterward, Terry Jo neither expressed anger at Julian Harvey nor ever explicitly stated the belief that he had killed her family.

She never saw him do anything violent and so, for those many years, she called it all "the accident."

After this second interrogation, Terry Jo was discharged from the hospital. The hospital had informed the press that she would be released in the afternoon, but she was spirited out of the hospital in the morning through a back door. Terry Jo drove to the airport with her aunt and uncle for a flight to Milwaukee to stay for a few days with another uncle, their tickets under assumed names. Terry Jo was heading home, although home would never be what it had been.

Terry Jo had spoken ill of no one, including Julian Harvey, since the *Bluebelle* tragedy, and she had been wonderfully supported by a great many people beyond family, friends, schoolmates – even by hundreds of complete strangers who wrote to her, some to tell her that they had named their newborn daughters after the bravest girl in the world. But one thing that added to her hurt after the *Bluebelle* tragedy was that there were a few people – very few in fact – who questioned the truth and accuracy of her story. It hurt that Mary Dene's brothers back in Wisconsin had raised questions about her first interview and were not convinced that their brother-in-law had lied. Terry Jo knew she had told the truth as far as she could know it.

After the second interview was made public, Mary Dene's brothers were satisfied that Terry Jo's account was the true one, not that of their late brother-in-law.

But it turns out they were leaning that way already. Dene's brother, Harry, now volunteered that Harvey had led Dene to believe before their marriage that he was well-to-do when, in fact, he was penniless and deeply in debt. Harry had evidently been doing a lot of research into Harvey's background since shortly after the *Bluebelle* tragedy, possibly even hiring a private investigator. "He conned her into thinking he was a big shot, when he was nothing but a bum," Harry had said.

Harry added that another thing he had learned was that Harvey once suggested to a friend that if he bought an airplane, Harvey could wreck it, make it look like an accident, survive the crash, and split the insurance proceeds with him. "Harvey had lots of experience wrecking planes and boats and coming out of them alive," he said.

Photo Credit: Jay Rimkus, *Miami News*

Terry Jo sits with a doll, given to her by the crew of the Captain Theo, *while recovering in a Miami Hospital in 1961.*

CHAPTER TEN

Terry Jo's Truth

There was a growing view that Harvey had committed murder. Harvey's friend, James Boozer, and others had serious doubts about his story of a devastating accident, making murder all the more likely. Harold Pegg, the *Bluebelle*'s owner, did not believe Harvey's story from the moment he heard it. Pegg, a swimming pool contractor, had come to sailing only recently, although he had dreamed of owning a sailboat for years.

Although he had purchased the *Bluebelle* only four months earlier, Pegg had researched boats thoroughly before buying the sailing vessel. Experienced in engineering and construction, he knew when something was well built, and he soon knew a lot about sailboats. Besides, he wanted to make certain that whatever boat he purchased would be a sound investment.

Pegg vehemently denied that the *Bluebelle*'s mainmast was defective and could have failed as Harvey claimed. He had had the boat thoroughly inspected and the masts were completely sound, except for some superficial softening of the wood in one small area of the mainmast that was repaired at a boatyard. Harvey knew about this repair and may have used it as the basis for his claim of failure. Previous owners also testified that the *Bluebelle* was a sound boat, including one who had ridden out a hurricane in it with no damage.

Pegg also did not believe that there had been a fire. First of all, the mast could not have fallen straight down as Harvey claimed. The wind that broke it would have pushed it over the side, carrying rigging with it. But even if a fire had broken out in the engine room, all Harvey had to do was pull a release right there in the cockpit. Harvey knew all about that release because Pegg had shown it to him several times. The *Bluebelle* was equipped with a state-of-the-art fire suppression system. There was a fixed CO_2 system – a large CO_2 bottle – in the engine room that could be quickly triggered by pulling the release in the cockpit close to the wheel. The CO_2 would instantly be drawn into the engine and kill it. It also would instantly fill the entire engine compartment and much of the bilge beyond, immediately depriving any fire of oxygen.

He also did not believe that Dr. Duperrault would have kept the boat headed into the wind, fanning flames right back at anyone in the cockpit. That made no sense to him. And, unknown by either Pegg or investigators at the time, Arthur Duperrault was an experienced sailor, and a man who had a clear head in a crisis.

As it turned out, Harvey told his story of a squall, broken masts, and fire to a surprisingly large number of people in the two days between being picked up by the *Gulf Lion* and testifying at the Coast Guard hearing. He either talked to or was overheard by nearly a half-dozen members of the *Gulf Lion* crew. Collectively they observed a number of things that might help to clarify what actually happened, what Harvey's state of mind was, and what his plan might have been.

The *Gulf Lion* captain noted that when Harvey climbed the rescue ladder, he was disheveled and barefoot, looking like a man who had abandoned a ship in desperate haste. While consistent with a sudden emergency, as Harvey claimed, collectively with other evidence it might suggest something else.

It was also interesting that Harvey twice told crew members that both Dr. and Mrs. Duperrault were killed outright by falling rigging, while he later told the formal hearing that the passengers were only injured. Harvey's several versions of events certainly suggest he was making things up as he went along, and was not telling a straight story.

Several *Gulf Lion* crewmen noted two additional things. First, that he didn't act like someone who had just lost his wife, but seemed inappropriately cool, and he never asked to send messages to his wife's family and relatives of the Duperraults. Second, that he seemed strangely anxious that a search might actually find survivors, and similarly anxious that there would have to be an official inquiry. He asked two or three crewmen whether they thought anybody might have survived, while otherwise arguing strenuously with the captain against a search by the *Gulf Lion* because it would be fruitless, saying he had already searched for hours. A couple of crewmen said he actually seemed relieved when they said no one could have survived in the water for long.

Two crewmen asked why Harvey had no blood on him, even though he said he had been surrounded by bleeding people in the cockpit. Harvey answered that seawater must have washed it off. They did not believe that a simple swim in the sea would wash blood out of clothes. In direct support of Terry Jo's account of no fire, the crewmen did not smell smoke on Harvey's clothes, or on her sister's body.

One crewman who examined the raft found flares sitting virtually in plain sight in a bag, seriously undercutting Harvey's later statement that he couldn't find flares. Crewmen got the impression that Harvey did not want to use flares that night because he had reason not to want to be found too close to where the *Bluebelle* went down – perhaps too close to any evidence of what really happened.

One crewman who helped bring René down to the ship's sick bay said that the body of the girl was still soft, too soft in his opinion for her to have died some twelve hours previously. This is only one layman's observation and opinion, but it raises the chilling implication that René might somehow have been alive initially with Harvey and that Harvey had drowned her later. It is hard to imagine how René could still have been alive, however, since Terry Jo never heard or saw any sign of her. It is also possible that René's body was flexible not because she had died recently but because rigor mortis had worn off and the warmth of the day had softened tissues.

As the *Gulf Lion* was closing in to pick up Harvey, one crewman reported something that intrigued investigators and that speaks to whether Harvey had a plan: He saw something red sinking slowly near the dinghy as the *Gulf Lion* got close. To him it looked like a standard gas can. This told Coast Guard investigators that Harvey might have had a small outboard (a "kicker") that he also threw overboard, as none was found. Several crewmen who examined the dinghy (which was retrieved along with the raft) also saw the marks of a motor on the stern of the dinghy, and at least two added that they looked fresh. The conclusion that Harvey had propulsion seems inescapable, as does the conclusion that he did not want that to be known. This suggests that he had a destination he was trying to reach, or at least that he wanted to go some distance before he was found.

It would have taken time for Harvey to discard both a kicker and a gas can after being spotted: The motor would have been relatively quick and unobtrusive – all he would need to do is unscrew the clamps and tip it over the back; the gas can would take longer because, in order to sink it, he would have had to pour out the gas and then hold the can under water while it slowly gurgled full with seawater. Meanwhile the *Gulf Lion* would be getting ever closer. Then, even full of seawater, a gas can would have enough neutral buoyancy that it would, in fact, sink slowly.

As far as Harvey having a means of propulsion (besides the dinghy's sail), there is another fact that did not receive a lot of attention in the hearing or documents: the Coast Guard record shows that Harvey traveled roughly eight miles in half a day. (This has to be a rough estimate because it isn't certain exactly what time the *Bluebelle* sank, nor precisely where it sank.) Terry Jo drifted roughly eighteen miles in three-and-a-half days. In other words, Harvey traveled nearly half as far as Terry Jo in one-seventh the time, a rate over three times that of hers. Since Terry Jo's time and distance define the drift rate resulting from wind and current alone, clearly Harvey had propulsion.

Further, since the raft behind the dinghy was virtually a sea anchor, Harvey was correct that wind pressure on the sail would tend to push the dinghy over rather than propel the tandem forward efficiently and safely. Harvey could have been right that he could not reasonably use the sail, except possibly in lighter winds.

Therefore the only way he could have traveled three times faster than Terry Jo is with a motor. On the other hand, he could not go far with only a can of gas and a tiny motor that might make one knot at best. So there is no way to be sure where he was headed or why, although it does seem he wanted to be found later rather than sooner, perhaps at a time of his choosing.

It is clear that he was headed roughly due west – possibly a little north of west – toward Florida, rather than southwest toward Great Stirrup Cay only eight or so miles away. Where was he headed? He certainly knew where Great Stirrup was (and it was conveniently equipped with a lighthouse to head to). And he certainly could tell direction from the stars overnight and then from the sun in the morning, not to mention from what he knew to be a generally southeasterly breeze.

It appears that Harvey hoped to be found later rather than sooner, possibly to make it harder to calculate where the *Bluebelle* had gone down and thus more difficult to find any debris or bodies. But was it also to make him look more like the beleaguered, indeed heroic, survivor? The longer he was at sea before he fired his flares, the more compassion and praise he would receive. Once he got closer to Florida, he would not have to worry about being picked up because there was a great deal of boat and small-plane traffic between the Bahamas and Florida to spot him. When he did decide to set off flares, he could then claim that a couple of other boats and planes just hadn't seen his earlier ones.

The crew of the *Gulf Lion* tended to respond to Harvey in one of two ways: while most of them were suspicious and saw through Harvey's story (one even said "there was something funny there"), two crewmen said that Harvey seemed a "damned decent fellow."

When the *Gulf Lion* transferred Harvey and the body of René to the harbor boat at Nassau so Harvey could fly back to Florida, the pilot boat skipper said that he saw "bruises on the child's forehead." This suggests that she, too, might have died violently as Terry Jo's testimony revealed that Jean and Brian Duperrault had.

The port director met Harvey when he was taken ashore in Nassau. Harvey handed him a statement about the loss of the *Bluebelle* he had written during the many hours he was on the *Gulf Lion*. The director said that the *Bluebelle* captain looked bedraggled. He was still wearing the salt-encrusted pants in which he had left the *Bluebelle*. The *Gulf Lion* crew had given him a clean shirt and shoes for his bare feet, but for some reason he had stubbornly refused to trade his salt-stained pants for better ones.

Harvey was taken to a hotel. One of the hotel staff who came into his room to help him settle in was startled to see that one of the beds was "covered with money – wet money that was drying out. I don't know how much there was, but I saw a fifty, lots of twenties and tens, fives, and ones. They covered the whole top of the bed." That must have been the reason Harvey would not give up his pants. Friends of Harvey's later shared, in fact, that he had a practice of splitting the lining of his pants and concealing large amounts of cash there. Large amounts of cash also suggest some kind of plan, and secretiveness.

By this time, the port director had read Harvey's statement and found, like others, that Harvey's story "had plenty of loopholes in it." He waited for Harvey to return and answer some follow-up questions, but the next morning Harvey went straight to the airport and flew to Miami.

Bahamian authorities decided to do an autopsy on René's body. The cause of death was found to be drowning. The medical examiner was unable to say, of course, if the drowning was accidental or intentional. He reported that he found bruises on the child's left elbow, but his report mentioned none on her forehead. But the finding along with no signs of trauma does little to clarify how Terry Jo's sister actually died.

René's body was sent to Green Bay. Weeks later some urged that the body be exhumed and a second autopsy be performed to check whether there were, in fact, bruises on René's forehead or other signs of trauma, and whether drowning had indeed caused her death. It is possible, of course, that what some on the *Gulf Lion* crew saw as bruises on René's forehead were just blotches of discoloration that can begin to form hours after death as unoxygenated blood pools in tissues.

While the reports of many who saw Harvey right after the *Bluebelle* tragedy undercut his story in various ways, there were two other stunning developments that spoke more directly to Harvey's state of mind and to what happened on the *Bluebelle*.

First, an anonymous telephone caller reached Mary Dene Harvey's brother, Harry Jordan, in Milwaukee and told him to "Check Traveler's Insurance, Miami." This anonymous call suggests that someone knew things about this case or about Harvey's personal affairs, but no such person was ever identified. A quick follow-up found that shortly before the *Bluebelle* voyage, Harvey had taken out a $20,000 policy on Dene's life, with himself as the beneficiary. It included a double-indemnity clause that meant a payoff of $40,000 (about $300,000 today) if she died accidentally. Possibly the caller was simply a concerned insurance company employee who tracked down Mary Dene's next of kin because he knew about Harvey's insurance policy and had read about the *Bluebelle* story in the press.

Then there was one final, powerful statement from Harold Pegg: He was curious about scratches he noticed on Harvey's right arm and hand when he saw him the evening after Harvey returned. "He told me they were wire cuts that he got them when he scrambled through the rigging that was tangled in the cockpit, while going after the cable cutters. But I've worked hard all my life and I know wire cuts when I see them." Then he added: "Those were fingernail scratches. Somebody fought him." Harry Jordan recalled that Mary Dene had very long fingernails.

In addition to ample evidence of suspicious and devious behavior, inconsistent and implausible accounts, and even lies, there is now evidence of a motive to murder – money. And there is additional evidence to bolster Terry Jo's report of physical violence. Coast Guard investigators concluded that the weight of the circumstantial evidence pointed to Harvey having engaged in a rampage of killing. They believed he left both Terry Jo and her sister below decks to drown. But Terry Jo never saw or heard René below decks. Surely she would have screamed or tried to escape the main bedroom where the water was rising if, in fact, that was where she was. Also, since René was still wearing her life vest, it was likely she was still topside when the killing happened.

One way to resolve some remaining questions at this great distance in time would be to locate the *Bluebelle* in the depths of the

Providence Channel and resolve, once and for all, any questions of the broken masts and major fire that Harvey claimed. The *Bluebelle* also could be searched for forensic evidence such as a knife, rifle, human remains, or human artifacts such as jewelry, wristwatches, etc., that might indicate where bodies once lay.

Concerning bodies, Terry Jo saw her mother and brother in the main cabin, but saw no sign of either her father or Mrs. Harvey. This might mean that the bodies of her father and Dene were in Harvey's forward cabin. It would make sense that Harvey would want, if possible, all of the bodies to be below decks so that none would float away, possibly to be found in a search.

It would not be that hard to get a rough idea of where the *Bluebelle* now rests. Knowing wind speed and direction, and direction of currents at that time in 1961, and knowing especially where Terry Jo was picked up and roughly what time the *Bluebelle* went down, searchers could reason back to where the yacht most likely sank. Terry Jo's position would be critical because it was only wind and current that moved her to where she was found.

Lacking forensic evidence, there might be more that can be gleaned from what is known beyond just inferring that Harvey was a mass killer. But reconstructing what happened is extremely difficult because, by the time the only witness woke up, all of the deaths were long over (with the possible puzzling exception of Terry Jo's sister). Yet Terry Jo did see two things that speak to Harvey's state of mind. When Harvey rushed at her, his eye was rolling hideously. Since this tic would occur when Harvey was under great stress, it suggests that he was agitated and acting in desperate haste, not carrying out some cold-blooded and calculated plan.

Another sign of haste is that Terry Jo saw the sails lying all over the deck. This means that Harvey had simply let them drop suddenly to bring the boat to a stop, and he let them lie because he was desperately occupied with getting ready to flee the *Bluebelle*. He would have needed the boat to be at a standstill so he could launch the dinghy and raft. This would also be necessary if there was no one to steer the boat.

The additional fact that Harvey had no shoes when rescued is another telling sign that he acted out of frenzy. It may be possible to infer one more thing: the reason for Harvey's agitation is that an initial plan that was coldly calculated – to kill only his wife – had blown up on him.

~~~~~

In order to see if the adult Tere (she changed her name when she was nearly a teenager to escape the "brave little Terry Jo" stigma) could recall any more details from that night that might be helpful, she agreed in 1999 to have sodium amytal administered under the direction of a psychiatrist. Sodium amytal is the latest version of "truth serum," and is regarded highly by some psychiatrists, not so highly by others. Tere was more than willing to try it because she recognized that her perception – and later recall – of things during the intense trauma of those awful moments might not have been fully accurate, and she might have actually seen things that did not fully register under so much stress. Tere also viewed this as a very important step in telling her story. It could be used not just to try to uncover more information, but also to directly face the question of whether what she testified to was, in fact, the truth. Tere faced this unflinchingly.

Sodium amytal is a sedative that works by relaxing a patient and, thereby, reducing inhibitions against recalling anxiety-provoking memories. Because it produces such a profound state of relaxation, it is often used in conjunction with hypnosis. Sometimes the subject is so relaxed that they are virtually in a hypnotic state already.

Tere's co-author of this book, a developmental psychologist with graduate clinical training, was present during the interview. When Tere was under the amytal, she was amazed at how fully she felt like she was Terry Jo again, "back there" on the *Bluebelle* and reliving that awful night. Her voice at times even sounded like that of a young girl, in pitch and inflection – the voice of Terry Jo. In this state, the psychiatrist asked her questions about what she saw and heard that night.

Two things were striking during this interview. First, Tere/ Terry Jo recalled very much the same things to which she testified. The main difference was that she had greater clarity and certainty on some things than during her original testimony. One was that it was indeed a rifle that Harvey held while standing in her doorway; another was that she, indeed, saw a knife along with blood on deck. She was absolutely certain there was no fire, and that the masts and rigging were intact. Her certainty about masts and rigging make the conclusion that there was no tragic accident all the more certain, too.

Second, Tere did recall a number of additional details that help to clarify the events of that night. (Not all of them came directly from the amytal interview; some emerged later.) She was able to recall that her mother was lying dead in her day clothes, not her pajamas, meaning that she must have been topside when the killing started. Brian, however, was in his pajamas, meaning he had come below to retire in his main cabin bunk. His screams, then, might not have been because he was being attacked, but rather that he saw his mother under attack and called for his father, whom he could not have known was probably already dead.

Tere also realized that the sound of splashing water she heard wasn't from the captain washing blood off the deck, but rather from water rushing into the boat from valves that had been opened in the engine room hull. Those valves must have been opened in the moments immediately after Terry Jo's mother and brother had been killed. This scenario is made more likely by this fact: the interior wall of Terry Jo's sleeping cabin was actually a lattice screen that could be removed, if needed, in order to gain access to the engine room from that side.

Under sodium amytal, Tere remembered that when she returned to her berth after being shoved back by Harvey, she could make out that the light in the engine room had been turned on. This could only have happened if Harvey was just there, immediately after he had killed the two in the cabin and while Terry Jo was sitting stunned, afraid, and confused on her berth.

Since the main entrance to the engine room was on the other side of the room from Terry Jo, it is entirely possible that she would not have heard him enter it. The only reason Harvey could have had to enter the engine room just then would have been to open valves to sink the boat. (He may have opened valves in the forward hull before that.)

When she was originally interrogated, Terry Jo had said that she heard "the engine running that night." As a result of the amytal interview she realized that the sound she heard that night decades ago was not, in fact, quite like the heavy pulsing sound of a piston engine but rather the lighter, whirring sound of an electric motor – the motor or motors of bilge pumps, perhaps. The smell of oil coinciding with what she first thought was the engine sound means that the bilge was filling up with water. The pump was running full time, its switches thrown by the rising floats designed to trip them. And it was right after hearing that "engine" sound that she noticed the water rising in her cabin.

It was only since the amytal interview that Tere had come to realize another important thing: that that hammering sound she heard shortly after Harvey left her doorway was too irregular to be "hammering" but actually was the uniquely hollow, vaguely drum-like sound that a small, light dinghy makes when it bangs randomly against the side of a boat. This meant that Harvey launched the dinghy right after he went up, right after standing in her doorway.

One final thing Tere recalled is that the "pail" she originally said she saw Harvey carrying on deck the first time she was there never did exactly look like a pail; it now looked to her mind's eye more like a gas can. This reinforces the view that the *Gulf Lion* crewman saw a sinking gas can.

It is possible that René was already below decks, asleep, when the killing began, but not likely. She would have had to have slept through the same commotion that woke her sister, and then remained in the main bedroom beyond the main cabin while the boat filled with water. Surely, wouldn't she have begun to scream at some point, or try to escape?

Terry Jo had also reported that René was in the cockpit wearing her life preserver when she went to bed that night, and René was wearing a life preserver when she was found with Harvey. It doesn't seem likely that Harvey would have somehow put a life preserver on her in the timeframe with which he had to work. The most likely scenario then is that René was topside with her mother and father.

René must already have been dead somehow and in the dinghy when Harvey handed Terry Jo the line. When it slipped out of Terry Jo's hands, he immediately dived in after it and disappeared into the darkness indicating, perhaps, that he had already placed René's dead body in the dinghy. It is, of course, possible that he did find her body in the water, but the area was pitch black the instant the *Bluebelle* went under as its lights shorted out.

Terry Jo had to be only yards away initially, just on the other side of where the *Bluebelle* had been. Terry Jo said she saw nothing, and heard nothing – no splashes such as those that might have been made by Harvey retrieving a floating body, or paddling around searching, and most importantly, no flashlight beams from the flashlight that Harvey had when he was picked up by the *Gulf Lion* – especially if he "circled" around where the boat had gone down. If he had circled, he likely would either have run into Terry Jo, or been seen or heard by her.

He likely did not search at all; he didn't even remain there. He hoisted sail right away and headed off in a predetermined direction. He did not then use the motor, because Terry Jo heard no such sound; plus it would have been hard to mount a motor in the dark. Also, if there were light winds, he could have sailed somewhat successfully towing the raft.

Why would Harvey, surprised by Terry Jo's reappearance on the deck of the sinking boat, hand her the line to the only means of saving his own life, the dinghy, when only seconds remained before the sailboat would be gone? Clearly he did not intend to take her with him and save her, as he had only minutes before left her below. The only reason he would have paused is that he intended to take a few seconds to grab some kind of weapon and kill her after all. Since she was no longer trapped below decks on a sinking boat, he decided in that split second to make absolutely certain that she would not survive. (This might be one source of his anxious questions about survivors.) He had been certain up to then that she would drown, trapped below decks in the sinking *Bluebelle*. When Terry Jo let the line to Harvey's means of escape slip away, it caused him to jump after the dinghy and, thus, saved her life yet one more time during that nightmare night.

Once Harvey got to the dinghy and turned and saw that the *Bluebelle* was gone, and all was silent, it is conceivable that he simply told himself that he had had no reason to worry after all because, below decks or not, and with no lifejacket, Terry Jo could not possibly survive for long in the water – if she hadn't drowned already, possibly tangled in the rigging or lines of the sinking ship. So he simply told himself to carry on with his escape.

The fact that Harvey had René's body with him tells two things: First, he intended to be picked up, otherwise why would he have kept René's body; second, he had to be absolutely confident that an autopsy would find that she died of drowning. The only conclusion then is that Harvey either knew she had drowned accidentally (hard to imagine in a mass killing scenario, unless she had been flung overboard by her mother in an instant of desperation to save her from the knife-wielding Harvey, in which case he could in fact happen to find her floating face down later); or perhaps she was knocked unconscious when Harvey came after her mother and (grim to contemplate) he drowned her at some point later, holding her head under water.

Here is a brief outline of how things might have happened based on all that is known (and deduced):

• Harvey, intending to kill his wife for the insurance and, therefore, wanting to make it look accidental, attempts neatly and quietly to kill – likely stab – his wife that night in the seclusion of their cabin, having left Dr. Duperrault at the helm, with his wife and younger daughter in the cockpit. His plan is to kill Dene, weigh down her body, surreptitiously slide her overboard when no one else is around, then come back to spend the rest of the night at the helm. In the morning he would go to their cabin and discover that she is "missing," somehow having fallen overboard during the night. His attempt goes awry and there is an altercation as Dene desperately fights, unsuccessfully, for her life – thus the scratches on Harvey.

• Arthur Duperrault hears the sound of the fight and rushes forward, only to confront a knife-wielding Harvey who quickly stabs him, killing him on the forward deck.

• Jean Duperrault rushes toward her husband, only to have Harvey turn on her. She rushes back to the cockpit, grabs René to protect her, only to have Harvey stab and wound her (Jean). In the process René was clubbed or falls and hits hard on her head. Meanwhile a wounded Jean Duperrault staggers or falls down into the main cabin. An agitated Harvey, his calculated plan in shambles, now knows only three things: that he has to eliminate witnesses, sink the boat to bury all evidence, and get away.

• The sound of his mother falling into the cabin, followed by a seemingly crazed Harvey – worked up by his orgy of killing – awakens young Brian. He screams for his father, having no idea that he is already dead.

• The commotion awakens Terry Jo, but she stays silent and frozen in her cabin for several minutes.

• Harvey quickly stabs Brian, and he falls next to his dead mother, their blood pooling on one side of the cabin floor, because the ship is tilting with no one at the helm.

• Harvey then quickly opens the entry to the engine room on the galley side of the boat, turns on the light, and hastily opens sea valves to begin to scuttle the boat. This is not especially noisy since he doesn't need to hammer holes in the hull or anything like that, and Terry Jo does not hear him. She also doesn't yet consciously observe that the light is dimly shining through the lattice screen wall on her side of the engine room.

• Harvey goes back topside to organize supplies for the raft and dinghy, both fixed to the top of the main cabin, and prepares to abandon the boat. He quickly drops the sails so that the boat is dead in the water, even though winds are fairly calm. He then throws Dr. Duperrault's body into the forward cabin, where Dene's body already is. (In the alternative, Dr. Duperrault's body may have fallen overboard in their struggle.) Harvey doesn't want to have any bodies float away as possible evidence if he can help it. He might also open valves in the forward cabin hull at this time. He is agitated now, doing all of this quickly and desperately. He won't have time to put on shoes. (The fact that he has no shoes does make it slightly more likely that he was in his own forward cabin when everything began – and quickly spun out of control.)

• As Harvey is feverishly pulling stuff together to leave, Terry Jo goes up into the cockpit after the shock of seeing her mother and brother below. She sees a knife and blood in the cockpit, and sails lying all over. She also catches Harvey in mid-preparation to leave, carrying a can of gas to put in the dinghy.

• Harvey, his eye rolling, pushes Terry Jo back down, and she returns in numb terror to her bunk and huddles for many minutes.

• Terry Jo hears the "hammering sound" that means that the dinghy has been launched and is banging into the boat, not that Harvey is banging holes in the hull. She also hears the sound of water splashing and "the engine running," which is actually the sound of the bilge pump. The two sounds together, plus the smell of oil, mean that water is rushing into the boat.

• Harvey goes below to retrieve the Duperraults' .22-caliber rifle from a main bedroom locker, and possibly looks quickly for any cash to grab.

• He then goes to Terry Jo's cabin, contemplates killing her, but decides she will drown anyway, and leaves.

• Terry Jo waits until water is waist deep then goes topside, only to be handed the dinghy line by Harvey. The captain is within seconds of fleeing the sinking boat, having loaded the dinghy and raft with supplies, including motor and gas.

• Terry Jo drops the line, Harvey dives off, and Terry Jo

Today, Tere is retired and spends her days in Kewaunee, Wisconsin, with her beloved dogs, Angel and Mickey (now deceased).

From left, Tere; daughter, Brooke Satrazemis, holding Tere's grand-daughter, Alison; son, Brian Hill, holding Tere's grandson, Wesley; aunt Janet Scheer; daughter, Blaire Morois; son-in-law, Jake Morois; and husband, Ronald Fassbender, gather for a happy get-together.

Terry Jo was rescued by the crew of the Captain Theo *after floating on a cork float for four days in the ocean.*

On September 5, 2009, Tere's daughter and son-in-law, Blaire and Jake Morois, named their newborn son Arthur after Tere's late father.

Tere, second from right, was raised by her Aunt Dot and grew up with her three cousins, from left, Greg, Dan and Jeff Scheer, after she lost her family.

heads for the float and toward a new life.

There is, however, a very different scenario that just might be possible: a Miami detective familiar with Harvey and his habits discounted the insurance-money motive for the *Bluebelle* killings. He was one of the detectives following up rumors about "Sinking, Inc." and the involvement of known Harvey associates in smuggling in and out of Cuba. He claimed to have uncovered clues that convinced him that the mass killing on the *Bluebelle* happened when Harvey rendezvoused with another boat in the dead of night to pick up a load of narcotics or other contraband he intended to smuggle into Florida.

Shortly before midnight on the fatal night, the detective believed, the *Bluebelle* sent out a radio call giving her position. He claimed to have received this information from a ham operator in the Bahamas, but the Coast Guard said it was unable to confirm any such call.

"As the transfer was being made, Duperrault came back on deck and walked right into the middle of it.

"Harvey panicked," the detective continued. "He struck Duperrault. The doctor ran and Harvey chased him and killed him. The other boat pulled away and Harvey was left with his problem. He killed the others to protect himself."

Although it seems improbable that Harvey would risk such a rendezvous at night with passengers on board (and, remember, Terry Jo earlier said that her father had wanted to stay on deck all night, and that Jean and René might stay there, too), subsequent and seemingly unrelated events have given some added credibility to this smuggling theory. In 1998 it was reported in Florida newspapers that the two sons of *Bluebelle* owner Harold Pegg had been involved in a major drug-smuggling operation for many years, dating back at least into the 1970s, though there was no evidence of activity before then. All told, the brothers had amassed a fortune of some $46 million that they secreted in various offshore accounts.

The problem with the botched drug-smuggling theory is that no evidence at all exists to corroborate it, and it is well known that serious drug smuggling was not yet underway in 1961. Nevertheless, investigators did clearly establish that the Pegg brothers had been using their charter-boat business as a cover for their smuggling, and that they did make their drops in and around the Bahama islands. So an earlier smuggling operation gone bad cannot be totally ruled out.

Perhaps there will always be a *Bluebelle* mystery. Certainly there will be much mystery surrounding who Harvey really was, and just what happened that fateful night.

The one thing that will never be a mystery is what the young girl on the raft was made of.

Terry Jo, as captured by a crewman aboard the Greek freighter Captain Theo, *just before she was rescued.*

Photo Credit: John Galanakis

CHAPTER ELEVEN

The Mask of the Hero

It is September 20, 1944. The war-weary B-24 Liberator comes in low and slow over the James River near Newport News, a flotilla of military boats filled with brass drawn up to observe. World War II is still raging, and brave men are still dying. Because some of those brave men are dying in B-24 ditchings, this is a test of the survivability of the high-wing four-engine Liberator in a water landing. The B-24 has a sorry history of breaking up and sinking when ditched, leaving too little time for crews to escape. This seems to be because the bomb bay doors collapse on impact, allowing tons of water pressure to explode into the plane, hammer the bulkhead at the back of the bomb bay, and violently pull the plane apart from front to back. This test plane has had its bomb bay doors and bulkheads reinforced, and the Army Air Corps needs to find out whether this will make it more survivable. The pilot and copilot have volunteered for this dangerous test.

The great lumbering machine slows to a near-stall speed of ninety-seven miles per hour and noses up slightly as its pilot skillfully flares out only feet above the water, eases the aircraft down, and planes the bottom of the aft section smoothly onto the surface. Within a second the drag on the rear of the bomber makes it nose up and slow down. In the next instant the wings lose all lift and the plane drops. The left wing catches water first, a split second before the B-24 noses in violently to a nearly 3G stop, pushing up a great wave. As the massive splash subsides and the plane wallows in the water, rescue boats rush up. Even after a skillful touchdown on smooth water and despite reinforcements to the fuselage, it is evident the bomber's back is broken and that this was truly a deadly dangerous exercise. The plane is literally bent in two, a great "V" in the water, both the nose and the aft section pointing toward the sky. So much for reinforcement.

But what of the crew? After a minute or two, the first of the brave volunteers, gray-haired copilot Col. Carl Greene, a twenty-eight-year veteran test pilot who first flew World War I biplanes, climbs out of the top hatch unharmed. After another long minute another survivor climbs out. It is the pilot, twenty-seven-year-old war hero Maj. Julian Harvey of the Army Air Corps, veteran of more than thirty bombing missions in B-24s and winner of the Distinguished Flying Cross for safely crash landing a shot-up B-24 after one of those missions. Once he is fully upright atop the plane, the strikingly handsome young pilot reaches into his shirt pocket. He pulls out a comb and runs it through his unruly, blond locks, as if to say that the worst thing this harrowing scrape with death did was muss up his hair. In one simple gesture he has told his war-besieged country, "You can count on me. I have what it takes. I will keep you safe." If he is also a little vain and conscious of his image for the cameras, it is easily forgivable in a hero so handsome and so brave and so real.

Such was the image that most people had of Julian Harvey, especially when they first met him: the American hero pilot, exceptionally skilled, extraordinarily brave, the embodiment of the cool and confident nonchalance in the face of death that is so much a part of America's image of its heroes. Here was the real deal, the guy John Wayne only pretended to be in the movies, except better looking. Many women and not just a few men looked at him and marveled at how a guy could be so exceptional: war hero, handsome, cool in a crisis, capable, dependable, confident.

But it is not hard to conclude that the very same Julian Harvey could have killed the people on the *Bluebelle*. And it is not hard to establish what his motive might have been: to kill his wife and claim her life insurance, apparently killing the others when his plan for cleanly and neatly disposing of her went awry, thus eliminating any witnesses.

The deeper "why" question goes to the kind of person Harvey really was. Clearly he wasn't quite what many people thought of him. There was something far darker behind the knight-in-shining-armor image.

But how did a glamorous and decorated war hero, a man who had risen from second lieutenant to lieutenant colonel in three short years in the Army Air Corps, a man of such skill and apparent courage and promise once tapped by top brass as a future leader, come to this end? Where had the darkness come from? One can begin to answer that question with the knowledge that, despite the attractive persona and magnificent feats of Julian Harvey, not everyone who had known him over the previous twenty years was entirely surprised at what apparently happened on the *Bluebelle*.

So who was Julian Harvey? He did not have an easy life in the beginning. He was born in 1917 in New York. His parents – his mother a chorus girl – divorced when he was one year old.

He lived alone with his mother until she married a well-known vaudeville producer when he was six. His stepfather was very generous, giving him a sailboat when he was about ten years old, and he loved sailing from that moment. He sailed often as a child and teenager, and even built his own sailboat. But when the double whammy of Hollywood and the Depression killed vaudeville, his mother and stepfather were abruptly impoverished and could no longer afford to raise him. They sent him to live with a well-off aunt and uncle in upscale Scarsdale, just outside of New York City, when he was about thirteen. The uncle by marriage was a prominent banker with a leading New York bank.

His aunt and uncle apparently doted on him, especially his aunt. He lacked for nothing during the Depression. But Julian still faced two large challenges when he was young: he was physically a weakling; and he had an embarrassing stammering problem whenever he was anxious or agitated, and a lazy eye that would become more pronounced for the same reasons.

On the other hand, he was uncommonly good looking and his aunt's pride and joy. In her eyes the boy could do no wrong. Embarrassed by his scrawny physique, a young teen Julian showed the kind of determination and dedication that would stand him well at times later in his life. He began to work with weights to build himself up. He soon became a superb physical specimen. This seems to have boosted his self confidence to the point where he felt more comfortable in social situations and was able to better control his stammering.

Although it seemed like Julian Harvey was growing into the kind of person who would not shy away from challenge and adversity, in his later teen years he learned that his uncommon good looks, plus his physique, meant that he didn't need to face one kind of teenage stress: asking girls out. They came after him. Years later, even after the *Bluebelle* story was everywhere, he was still remembered by former female classmates – indeed, by a legion of other women as well – as dreamy, and gorgeous, and sweet. They could not imagine that the Julian Harvey they remembered could be a killer. Former male classmates remembered him as a skilled and graceful athlete, especially in boxing and gymnastics, and a bit of a show-off.

One result of Harvey's charms was a very early marriage while he was still in high school. His aunt and uncle managed to get it annulled within a year.

Harvey graduated from Great Neck High School in Long Island, New York, in 1937. The first job he found was in door-to-door sales. Unfortunately, this proved to be outside of his comfort zone. According to his younger sister, when a woman answered the first door he knocked on, he became so nervous that he stammered fiercely. Humiliated, he fled.

Clearly, interaction with customers could unnerve him. But in other potentially high-stress situations he showed remarkable cool, such as the time he calmly walked into the living room and suggested quietly that his grandmother might want to go for a walk. Then he returned and just as calmly got his mother. His motive, it turned out, was that the house was on fire and Julian did not want the women to panic.

Not liking the stress of sales, Harvey – in a move that might have helped influence how he lived the rest of his life – decided he would capitalize on his looks and physique. It wasn't long before he was hired as a male model for the famous Powers agency. He worked there for a year or so.

In 1939 he entered the University of North Carolina to pursue engineering. He had shown an aptitude for this field in his study of boats and in building his own sailboat. The next year he transferred to Purdue. He had completed two years of college by the summer of 1941. By this time, everyone was saying it was only a matter of time before the United States would be in the war in Europe, and possibly taking on the expansionist Japanese in the Pacific as well. Rather than waiting to be drafted to serve as a lowly slogging foot soldier, Julian decided in August 1941, as a twenty-four year old, to join the Army Air Corps. (There was, as yet, no U.S. Air Force.) "That's where the glory is," he told some friends, in an early suggestion of how important glamour and image would be to him.

Harvey applied to Air Corps cadet training, providing glowing letters of recommendation from Purdue faculty. Those letters were so effusive in their praise of him that some wondered whether they might have been fabricated by Harvey himself, but there was no hard evidence of this and the Army had far too few resources to follow up on such questions. And they needed qualified personnel. With his engineering training and sailing background, Julian was indeed qualified, and he did exceedingly well as an air cadet, showing exceptional drive and talent for flying. He graduated as a skilled pilot and was commissioned as a second lieutenant, with a promising military future ahead of him. In the meantime, while he was in training, war had broken out, putting an even greater premium on promising young officers.

Even though Harvey had first trained in 1930s-era biplanes, his first assignment was to fly four-engine B-24 bombers. He was a quick study in learning to fly the great beasts and soon was flying anti-sub patrols along the southern East Coast from a base in Florida, looking for Nazi subs that were torpedoing coastal shipping on a daily basis. Many Americans have forgotten that in the earliest days of the war, the front lines were just off our beaches. There is no record of Harvey having engaged any subs, but there is a record that on one of his breaks from flying he attended an upscale social event where young officers mingled with young socialites. There the handsome aviator, resplendent in his dress uniform, met a beautiful seventeen-year-old debutante named Ethel Fohl who was from a wealthy south Florida family. She was smitten and fell for him immediately, she said. A few months later they were married.

Years later, after the *Bluebelle* case had flooded the papers, Ethel told reporters at the time she had never met anyone who came so close to matching her image of the ideal man, and she had been captivated by the pilot from central casting with such an abundance of boyish charm. She was also taken by his worldliness and his dynamic personality, but looking back she realized that she saw him through very young eyes. She did note that even back then, she could tell that he was "terribly egotistical" and "so proud of his beautiful body." But even though they had divorced years earlier and she had seen his cold side, she still could not believe that Julian could be a killer.

In the fall of 1942, Harvey was ordered overseas. He spent seven months in England flying B-24s across the English Channel on bombing missions over Europe. On one mission his plane was badly shot up, but rather than having his crew bail out, he managed to fly it back to England and land it safely. His entire crew survived. His superiors regularly wrote excellent reports on his actions, but some of his colleagues began to see him as accident prone because he had at least two other crash landings.

In 1943 he was transferred to Libya to fly missions across the Mediterranean against Nazi-controlled southern Europe. He was one of the pilots slated to fly in the famous and, ultimately, very costly raid on the Ploesti oil fields in Romania. However, official records of that raid show that Harvey's B-24 *Hellsadroppin* aborted and returned to Libya because of "engine trouble."

It was not the first time that Harvey had aborted a mission, leading to scuttlebutt about him among fellow pilots, but drawing no official notice from superiors. Perhaps they thought he was from central casting, too. Harvey completed some thirty missions altogether, and by January 1944 he was back in the States, at Eglin Field in Florida. Because he had shown great skill as a pilot, especially in that one remarkable crash-landing of a severely wounded aircraft, he was chosen to work as a test pilot helping to improve the aircraft in which young American men were flying, and dying.

While Harvey had been overseas, his wife, Ethel, had given birth to a baby boy she named Julian Jr. Shortly after the baby was born, she had taken him to live for a time with Julian's aunt. She ended up staying there only two weeks because the woman made it clear that Ethel was not nearly good enough for her beloved and perfect nephew. Devastated and angered by this experience, she moved out and into a small apartment to raise her son alone.

Despite their having a child together, Julian abruptly informed his wife shortly after his return that he no longer loved her and wanted a divorce. She could keep the baby. Their divorce was final in early 1945.

So, Harvey became a bachelor again as he took up his assignment as a test pilot. It was on this assignment that he ditched the B-24 bomber for an audience. For this feat he received the Air Medal, adding still more luster to the image of Julian Harvey, the war hero. It struck some as odd, however, that immediately after the ditching, Harvey asked to be transferred from bombers to fighters.

Some other pilots wondered whether the ditching, in the end, had been too close for comfort and that Julian Harvey, who already had avoided some of the most harrowing missions he should have flown, had finally begun to lose his nerve completely. The ditching wasn't just a glamorous feat; he could have died. These same pilots were among those who viewed Harvey as egotistical and more concerned with the glory and glamour than with the job at hand. One of his fellow pilots at the time, who was also assigned to the test ditchings of B-24s, said of Harvey,

"Because of his wartime record in those early days, his good looks and his many decorations, he had a very egotistical air. He wore the special-cut Eisenhower jacket, pearl-pink chino trousers, and a yellow scarf. ... Harvey was considered a hero and no one challenged him in his wearing of his unconventional uniform."

Source:
National Advisory Committee for Aeronautics
(NACA - predecessor to NASA) Oral History Project

The note not only tells of Harvey's self-centeredness, but also alludes to the power his image and reputation had over others. That same pilot went on to note that some even doubted Harvey's story about his safe crash landing, although that does seem to be a matter of record – and no one ever questioned that Harvey was an extremely skilled pilot.

After the test-pilot assignment, Harvey was transferred a few times to other bases on a number of assignments, including a very brief stint on Okinawa immediately after the end of the war. He also was promoted to temporary lieutenant colonel and assigned to an administrative job in the Pentagon. He was soon restless "flying a desk" and asked for Air Force support to finish his college degree. So he went back to Purdue as an active Air Force officer for two more years, graduating with a bachelor's degree in Aeronautical Engineering in 1948.

By this time, Julian was thirty-one and had been single for three years. Ever active in the dating scene, he met yet another socialite, twenty-one year old Joan Boylen. After another very brief courtship, they married. Their son, Lance, was born in late 1948. Meanwhile, Harvey was transferred yet again, this time back to Eglin Air Force Base on the Florida panhandle. Married or not, it was well known around Eglin that Harvey continued to have affairs with many women. Joan told friends at the time that she knew about them but she still loved Julian, even though he showed a frightening flash of temper the one time she brought up his philandering.

Then, on April 21, 1949, Harvey was driving back to base from town on a rainy night with his wife and mother-in-law after seeing a movie. Harvey told officers afterward that despite driving very carefully, at about forty miles per hour, when he drove onto a narrow, old wooden bridge over a deep bayou, for some odd reason the car swerved sharply to the right. He said he cut hard back to the left and the car struck the left bridge railing, rolling and turning upside down as it went up and over the railing. The car dropped, twisting into twenty feet of cold, murky water, and sank immediately.

While the car was still rolling over in the air, Harvey said later, he was able to open the door and jump out, landing in the water. He swam to safety, but his wife and mother-in-law never surfaced, trapped in the sinking car.

Other people stopped at the scene minutes later. They later said that Harvey was seen simply standing on the bridge watching as others dived in to search for the two women. They noted that he talked in an oddly calm way as he stood watching the search, and they were shocked that this fit young man wasn't helping. Instead he seemed to be boasting when he told how easy it was to get out of the airborne car because he had so much experience escaping from wrecked airplanes. People who talked with him also sensed a complete lack of any strong feelings over the loss of the women, echoing the comments of some who observed Harvey after the *Bluebelle* incident years later. He seemed only to talk about himself.

Harvey had said he had opened the door and jumped out while the car was in the air. Yet two divers who went down to retrieve the bodies found all the doors closed but the driver's window was down. To them and others this indicated that Harvey had not gotten out by opening the door while airborne, as he boasted, but had ridden the car down, rolled the window open, and swam out when the car was under water, not even bothering to assist his wife and mother-in-law. This apparent lie by Harvey caused many to wonder if the incident had been a deliberate act staged to look like an accident. But even more telling was the fact that a vigorously healthy Harvey simply swam away and made no effort to save the two women in the critical seconds after the crash, or even later while he watched others jumping in to try to help.

The next day his wife's distraught father came to the base commander's office demanding an investigation, flat out accusing Julian of murder. But investigators found no evidence that would stand up in court, and there were ambiguities as to whether the matter fell under civil or military jurisdiction. So once again, Harvey had shown he was good at surviving wrecks – and possibly staging them – and once again, nothing derogatory was entered into his record. Shortly thereafter he collected on his wife's life insurance.

In the wake of the car crash and all the questions surrounding it, a military doctor at Eglin became curious about Harvey and talked to him informally a few times, trying to get a feel for his character. He was not assigned to do an official inquiry. He concluded in 1949 that underneath Harvey's veneer of charm and sophistication was an amoral man with no real empathy for others, a man who could be dangerous. In other words, a possible sociopath. So more than a decade before the *Bluebelle*, someone had seen a darker side of Harvey's persona. But the military doctor was not a psychiatrist and nothing regarding his views ever was entered in Harvey's record.

Within weeks of the death of his wife Joan, Harvey was living with another woman.

In 1950, Lieutenant Colonel Julian Harvey was transferred to Randolph Air Force Base in San Antonio, Texas. Here he soon met a young Texas businesswoman named Jitty. After a few months, she too accepted his proposal of marriage even though she, too, saw that he was vain and self-centered. They were married in late 1950. Interviewed by reporters a year after the *Bluebelle* tragedy, she not only spoke of his egotism, but also said that Harvey could show a violent temper. A friend who witnessed one outburst actually told her that she was concerned that Jitty might not be safe with him. Jitty also commented on Harvey's constant working out. "He loved only himself," she told reporters. Although she was his fourth wife, she said she had been led to believe that she was only his second.

Around this time, something seemed to have been happening, however, to the formerly confident Julian Harvey, according to his fourth wife. Harvey, who had seemed so self-assured in the past, was beginning to appear less confident and more awkward at Air Force social occasions, especially around superior officers. His stammering started again. Looking back, Jitty wondered if the B-24 ditching had been too powerful a reminder that he was a mere mortal, and the drowning of his previous wife, Joan, made him worry that he might be discovered.

Three months after Jitty and Julian were married, Julian was transferred to Korea to fly Sabre jets, as he had requested. When he returned two years later, after flying 114 combat missions in Korea, he told Jitty exactly what he told his second wife, Ethel, years earlier: "I don't love you anymore." In 1953 Julian and his fourth wife were divorced on the grounds of incompatibility. The secretary in his divorce lawyer's office said he had actually asked her for a date when he came to see the lawyer. The secretary said she accepted because "he was one great big gorgeous hunk of man." She added that she declined a second date, however. "Something about him made me uneasy."

As Jitty reflected on the Harvey she had known, her life with him, and the *Bluebelle* story, she told a reporter at the time, "I guess I am lucky to be alive." She added that, despite his egotism and bad temper, she never suspected that he could be the kind of person he evidently turned into on the deck of the *Bluebelle*. "Anyway, he didn't have me insured," she added, wryly.

It turned out that, as early as 1951, many of Harvey's Air Force colleagues were concerned that when he was sent to Korea that he was, or was becoming, psychologically troubled. But no one sensed that he could be dangerous. It was more a matter of Harvey appearing uncharacteristically fearful and anxious. In Korea he no longer showed the same bravado and cool confidence he had displayed when he ditched the B-24 – although he had, in fact, been able to avoid some of the most dangerous bombing missions as early as 1943 in World War II.

As it happened, he also avoided some combat situations in Korea. On some occasions when his flightmates engaged MIGs in dogfights, he claimed engine trouble and broke for home. He showed a marked lack of assertiveness in other situations, failing to take on MIGs when he had the chance. He also was on record as having three dead-stick landings (landings when his engine was out) in Korea. On 114 missions, he had many more "engine failures" than any of his peers, although his superiors never made any formal note of it. While his superiors wrote commendations lauding his skill in bringing planes back safely with no engine, his peers talked to each other about how he would deliberately cut his engine when he knew he could glide safely back to base. But he was still a highly skilled pilot, and he still knew how to make himself look good. There had developed a continuing pattern in Harvey's career of impressing his superiors while raising the eyebrows of his peers.

Harvey was also struggling when it came to continuing to make himself look good in his command role. He was a lieutenant colonel, but when he briefed lower-ranking officers under his command, he frequently stammered again. Harvey even asked a subordinate to write speeches for him, which he delivered – stiffly. He was so awkward that some of his men could not avoid laughing nervously. No one dared question him directly, however, or go over his head to his superiors, for fear he could ruin their careers. And everyone – superiors, peers, and subordinates – still saw Harvey through the lens of his status as decorated war hero; thus, the fact that he might be "losing it" never got the attention of superiors during most of Harvey's tour in Korea.

When Harvey left Korea in mid-1953, it had become clear that he had, at the very least, severe anxiety problems. He exhibited facial muscular tics, a rolling right eye, and stammering to the point that many now were seriously aware of his problem with "nerves."

Still, Harvey was a decorated war hero, and the Air Force tries to treat its heroes well, sometimes giving them more leeway than other officers. That may have gotten in the way of Harvey being seen more objectively earlier on. In any case, once his problems were recognized, if not fully understood, he was relieved of flight duty and "kicked upstairs" as a staff officer for a time at the

Pentagon. His performance drew no special recognition, and at least one fellow officer called it "undistinguished."

For years there were those who knew Harvey less well who still saw him as a World War II hero and brave test pilot. It seems that, for many years, people were seeing one of two Julian Harveys. One was Harvey, the handsome and charismatic shining knight who fearlessly flew right into the face of death, looked it square in the eye, and then smirked and nonchalantly combed his hair. This was the persona that the public and casual acquaintances knew, and that his superiors saw and commended.

The other was the darker Julian Harvey, hiding behind the mask – vain and arrogant, given to fits of rage, and periodically cruel to his wives. He seemed to be doing constant battle with the fears and anxieties that threatened to undermine the knightly image built on his successes and achievements, and constantly struggling to cover his insecurities and keep control of his humiliating stammering problem. This other persona was seen by his peers, but not his superiors; by his wives, but not by legions of other women who were attracted to him, or his casual acquaintances. It was observed by some experts early on – but by others, not at all.

In Washington, the glamour-boy Harvey was still robust enough to win his fifth wife: Georgiana was yet one more woman of substance. Harvey's reputation, charm and looks all still worked for him. Georgiana, who spoke six languages, had a strong personality. The result was, by all accounts, a stormy relationship. Unlike Harvey's earlier wives, she seems not to have stayed dutifully at home while Harvey philandered – which he still did. Harvey, still stationed in Washington, decided that now would be a good time to pursue another love. He wanted to fulfill his lifelong dream and become a sailor and ship master, perhaps with an eye toward a second life after retirement. In 1954, he and his wife bought the old, sixty-eight-foot yawl *Torbatross*.

Within a year, with Harvey at the helm, the *Torbatross* ran aground on the wreck of the World War I battleship *Texas* in Chesapeake Bay. The *Torby* sank. Since the battleship was a wreck for which the Coast Guard, and therefore the federal government, was responsible, Harvey sued for damages alleging that the wreck was not adequately marked. After a prolonged and controversial court case, Harvey won a settlement of $14,258 along with collecting on the insurance he took out on the *Torby*.

The *Torbatross* case seemed straightforward and that would have been the end of it except that, after the case was decided, acquaintances who were with Harvey on the boat at the time of the grounding said the wreck of the *Texas* was, in fact, marked well. They had to admit that in their view, Harvey had run into it intentionally. One of the Coast Guard officers investigating this case was Robert Barber, who was later involved in the *Bluebelle* case. He was certain when interviewed in 1992 that Harvey had rammed the wreck of the *Texas* deliberately, but a court decided differently.

At about the same time as the loss of the *Torbatross*, Harvey was sent back to Eglin Air Force Base near Pensacola, Florida, as deputy commander of the 3243rd Fighter Test Group. He also was to be a senior test pilot after lobbying hard to fly again. He had not liked desk duty, and he seemed to his superiors to once again be his old confident self. He appeared ready to be back on flight status.

As luck would have it, on one of his first flights in January of

1957, while flying the latest-generation F-86H Sabre, Harvey had an engine flameout (apparently entirely real). He had to eject. His chute opened with a powerful yank that severely injured his shoulder. While Harvey was recovering, many noticed that his facial and muscular tics and his stammering had returned with a vengeance.

While at Eglin, he and Georgiana bought the eighty-one-foot yawl *Valiant*, using proceeds from the *Torbatross* settlement. They sailed it around the Gulf Coast while Harvey recuperated. Being at sea and living his dream of the sailing life seemed to help Harvey recover from his injuries, and from the stress and anxiety that had provoked his tics and stammering.

Looking once again like the capable and reliable Julian Harvey that fit his hero knight reputation, Harvey was transferred to Edwards Air Force Base in California, which was becoming the site for the testing of the latest and hottest jets. Harvey, however, was assigned to be Special Assistant to the Commander of the 6515th Maintenance Group, not a flying assignment. Although Harvey was now at the hottest place for jet jockeys who had the "right stuff," his superiors decided they were not going to take the chance of putting him through the stresses of being either a full-time pilot or a commander of pilots. But they did want other younger hotshots to have the example of genuine hero around, even if he was semi-retired. As far as the younger pilots were concerned, Harvey had long since paid his dues to the gods of flight and to the Air Force.

Even though he was no longer on full-time flight status, Harvey still flew occasionally so he could keep his flight certification – and draw flight pay, a bonus given to every pilot as long as he flew a minimum number of hours. So, some time in early 1958,

Harvey, with a younger flyer as copilot, went for a flight in a T-33 trainer, a very reliable and forgiving plane to fly. As it turned out, however, this plane also had an engine failure and both pilots had to bail out. The bailout was far from routine, however, as the canopy would not detach. Harvey struggled to restart the engine and get control of the plane.

Finally, as they approached a dangerously low altitude, Harvey ordered his copilot to eject through the Plexiglas canopy (a riskier but engineered-for contingency in an ejection scenario). The copilot did so safely, the back of his ejection seat shattering the Plexiglas as it is designed to do and, in the process, knocking the entire canopy free. Harvey bailed out after him. The copilot landed safely, but Harvey was again seriously injured, hitting a piece of farm equipment when he landed. When he was picked up by a military ambulance, he was in great pain and screaming hysterically.

This reaction was completely out of character for a hero like Harvey, and was far beyond the previous muscular tics, anxieties, and stammering. It was a sign he had really lost it this time. He raged about how his entire life had been too violent and that he had had everything happen to him that could happen to a pilot besides get killed. "I am sick of it!" he screamed.

In the hospital he was treated for severe anxiety and given sedatives to control the anxiety and the severe twitching that now seemed to plague his entire body. While in the hospital, Harvey finally admitted to a couple of his colleagues that he actually began, as he put it, to "crack up" in 1952 in Korea. This was the same time that some of his peers were seeing signs of psychological problems and so many of his fellow pilots were noting he was beginning to avoid really engaging in air combat.

In March of 1958, Harvey was given a medical discharge from the Air Force with a pension based on the rank of major, since his rank of lieutenant colonel had never been made permanent. He was to receive a pension of half his base pay as a major. Harvey was furious. He refused to accept that arrangement and took his protests up the chain of command. Finally, he managed to get a retirement package where he would receive 60 percent of his base pay as a lieutenant colonel, even though he had never held that rank permanently.

Julian Harvey, decorated war veteran, former brave pilot and Air Force poster boy, then turned his back on the Air Force – except for continuing to benefit from his image and reputation – and looked toward fulfilling his lifelong dream to sail, have his own sailing yacht, and live his life at sea. He spent as much time as he could with Georgiana and his son, Lance, on his boat, the *Valiant*. However, this marriage was on the rocks, and in 1958 Georgiana sued for divorce, citing extreme mental cruelty.

While the divorce case was pending, Harvey took the *Valiant* to Cuba. A few miles offshore, it burned and sank. Harvey was picked up by a passing boat. He told how a fire broke out that quickly became a raging inferno and he barely escaped. Once again there was an insurance claim and a ruling in favor of Harvey. But years later one of Harvey's friends chuckled over the incident.

"Julian told the Coast Guard a beautiful story," he said. "He was a real expert at story-telling, because he had had so much experience talking himself out of trouble. He told me he set the fire himself because he was in a financial jam and needed the insurance money."

Since the *Valiant* also had caught fire some months earlier in the marina, but a passerby spotted it and put it out, there was more than a little suspicion of Harvey.

Harvey used this settlement to buy the seventy-foot schooner *White Swan* and begin a lucrative charter business to the Bahamas. Along the way he took another trip to Cuba. There were rumors after this trip that Harvey had smuggled guns and ammunition to Fidel Castro. No official records back this up, however.

Meanwhile, Georgiana was in court seeking a final divorce settlement. She claimed that in addition to extreme mental cruelty, Julian had simply come home one day and announced, much like he had to other wives, "I don't love you anymore. I don't want you to live on the boat with me anymore. Go get a divorce." They separated in June 1958, and were finally divorced in 1959.

For reasons not entirely clear, Harvey sold the *White Swan* in 1959. He worked as a deckhand for a while on the windjammer *Polynesia*. He also traveled to California for a few months and looked for sailing opportunities there. Back in Florida, Harvey soon began to figure in still more rumors around the Miami sailing community.

At the time, insurance investigators were gathering evidence on a boat-sinking racket that had cost their companies several million dollars. The racket involved owners "leasing" their craft to men who arranged for them to sink "accidentally" so the owners could collect the insurance. Some boat owners reportedly made dual deals with men who made additional big money running refugees from Castro's Cuba. The men would make several trips to

Cuba to bring out well-to-do refugees, then sink the boats before they became too well known to the Coast Guard, customs and police.

It was a lucrative racket for all concerned because it was easy to insure a boat for far more than it is worth. One insurance investigator, looking into what law enforcement came to call "Sinking, Inc.," said that "everywhere we went, we were always running into [the name of] Julian Harvey. He was a known companion of many of the suspicious characters. He was associated with owners and workers on boats that were apparently sunk for profit."

These investigations, plus the suspicious endings of both the *Torbatross* and the *Valiant*, meant that Harvey was coming under greater suspicion and scrutiny from law enforcement even before he met his sixth wife-to-be, Mary Dene Jordan, and before the Duperraults arrived in Fort Lauderdale.

It is tempting to suggest a "diagnosis" of Julian Harvey. From what is known, he showed signs of both sociopathic-personality disorder and narcissistic-personality disorder. Both types show a lack of real empathy with others, as Harvey did. Since a sociopath does not care what others think of him and a narcissist does, and since a narcissist has exaggerated self-importance, the diagnosis would lean toward narcissistic-personality disorder. But rather than argue for one diagnosis over the other, it might be sufficient simply to point out that a similar debate took place over the infamous serial killer Ted Bundy. He, too, was uncommonly handsome, disarmingly charming, and had an easy way with the ladies.

Rather than attempting an after-the-fact diagnosis, let it be said that it seems clear from Harvey's biography that he hid a great deal behind his handsome and charming persona – all his anxieties, insecurities, weaknesses, and darker impulses. Over time he learned how far he could get and how much he could get away with if he simply counted on still being able to win over people with his looks, his heroic reputation, and his charm. He kept getting away with more and more, until an innocent girl who happened to have one thing that Harvey lacked, namely integrity, simply told the truth.

Harvey's handsome mask was no longer enough to win the day. And he knew it. He left the *Bluebelle* hearing for that motel room because he also knew, far more painfully than anyone else, that while once there had been real promise behind a handsome face, now there was only hollow darkness.

CHAPTER TWELVE

All the Women Are Strong

If the story of Julian Harvey up to the time of slaughter aboard the *Bluebelle* and his subsequent bloody suicide is a chronicle of how a man who once "had everything" began to fall apart as he slowly descended toward a rendezvous with his own darkness, the story of Terry Jo after the *Bluebelle* is the chronicle of how a girl who had lost everything to that same darkness struggled to slowly put her life together. One relied on a glamorous image rather than inner substance; the other would rely on what she had inside, to hell with glamour and image. Harvey learned after it was too late that relying on a glamorous shell did not work; Terry Jo learned right at the get-go that she was made of tough stuff.

Terry Jo's challenge wasn't to put her life back together, because there weren't even pieces to reassemble. Her old life was shattered, the pieces of it strewn across – and under – the seas. She really was a female Moses in the bulrushes, a waif cast adrift on the waters who would begin her life all over again, almost from scratch. If anyone thought that Terry Jo's solitary ordeal was over when she left the hospital physically strong and fit, and headed back to Green Bay with her loving aunt and uncle, they were wrong. Rather, a long new chapter of lonely struggle was just beginning. The inner substance that helped see Terry Jo through a night of unspeakable horror and then days of peril on the sea would be tested over and over again.

It is hard, maybe wrong, to use the word "miracle" when five out of six innocent people die horrible deaths and one person survives. And yet Terry Jo's ordeal and survival were still extraordinary. Terry Jo drew strength – great strength – from the fact that she had survived. From the very first moment she was convinced that she must have survived for a reason. She had survived the worst there is. Even at the age of eleven, she wanted others to be inspired by that.

The word "extraordinary" in describing her survival is not an exaggeration. Terry Jo probably never reflected on it directly, but from the moment she woke up that unspeakable night until the time she left the hospital about two weeks later, her life had been spared or saved no less than eight times:

1) When the skipper Harvey was apparently too preoccupied with killing others and with preparing to abandon the *Bluebelle*;

2) When Harvey looked at her from her doorway, rifle in hand, but for whatever reason chose not to shoot her;

3) When Terry Jo let the line to the dinghy slip through her fingers, forcing Harvey to dive into the sea to chase after the dinghy, when he might have killed her;

4) Perhaps the most extraordinary, when she just managed to escape from the sinking *Bluebelle* onto the float;

5) When predators did not come after her because of the oil that coated both her and the float;

6) When she managed to get back onto the raft after falling from it while asleep at night;

7) When the *Captain Theo* picked her up; and

ALONE

8) When doctors saved her life in the hospital.

There is a profound paradox at the heart of the story of how Terry Jo coped with the initial horror and terror on the boat, and then escaped from it and the wild-eyed captain; and then with the solitary ordeal of floating utterly alone for four days. The two ordeals, one coming on the heels of the other, somewhat canceled each other out emotionally. The fact that she was numb with the shock of what she had just gone through at the moment she climbed onto the float actually served to insulate her from realizing fully what she was now up against. She continued as she sat on that float to feel some detachment and unreality as if she was still somewhat outside of herself observing what was happening.

Similarly – and the other side of the paradox as it were – the four days Terry Jo floated alone in her second ordeal gave her a new preoccupation that served, in turn, as a buffer against the full emotional impact of the initial horror and terror. The new ordeal occupied her enough that she didn't have "room" to dwell on what had happened on that boat.

She also had the following things going for her:

• She was young and healthy;

• She was lucky (not to be attacked by predators, and to be seen by the *Captain Theo*);

• She was blessed with a low-key temperament and, therefore, did not overreact to her situation, more or less accepting that she was where she was – she did not exhaust herself with hysterics;

• She never believed she was going to die and she never doubted that she would survive;

• She was already a bit of loner, used to being by herself;

• She showed what others have shown – she began over time to get used to even her extraordinary situation and accept it as a new norm;

• In the games she played as a child alone in the woods she had actually rehearsed being in solitary survival situations, so she had some emotional inoculation against her plight.

Terry Jo returned to Green Bay on November 30, 1961, to live with her aunt and uncle and their three sons, to see her friends again, and to go back to school. She returned to Green Bay quietly, just as she had left Miami secretly so that she wouldn't encounter the press. It had been arranged for her to live with her Aunt Dot and Uncle Ralph Scheer and their three sons. Her grandmother, Jenny Mae Duperrault, lived in an apartment attached to the Scheers' home, and Terry Jo took a bedroom in her grandmother's apartment.

She met first with relatives and later with her best friends. One of them gave her a kitten, and the local press was permitted a picture (but no questions) of a smiling Terry Jo with her girlfriends, and the kitten. Terry Jo had always loved and cared for animals.

One of the first things Terry Jo did was to answer, with the help of her relatives, the hundreds of letters that came in from around the world. Many of these letters are offers to be pen pals, including one from a boy in France named Jean-Jacques. There also were hundreds of gifts (dolls, stuffed animals, Bibles), and hundreds of inspirational letters, or letters that simply extend best wishes – and a few crackpots that were screened out by Terry Jo's aunt and uncle. Several letter writers would stay in touch for years.

Terry Jo would be much loved and have a secure home with her aunt and uncle. They were her legal guardians. As part of her adjustment to her new life, Terry Jo acknowledged her closeness to her new adoptive parents by coming up with new, more intimate names for them. She called them "Mo" and "Unk" – loving, yet emotionally distinct from "Mom" and "Dad." But in the months and years after the *Bluebelle*, her grandmother, Jenny Mae Doyle Duperrault, was especially close to her. She had been "Gammie" since Terry Jo's brother Brian first called her that as a baby. It was she who would teach Terry Jo life skills like sewing and knitting, and also a deep love of reading, including authors such as Taylor Caldwell, R.F. Delderfield, Pearl Buck, and others. The two of them spent many quiet evenings sitting together quietly reading books.

Even though Gammie had lost a son, two grandchildren, and a beloved daughter-in-law, she never brought it up in front of Terry Jo. Nor did she ever complain about the chronic poor health that limited her activities. A woman who was deeply religious and equally kind, she quietly and uncomplainingly shouldered the task of always being there for young Terry Jo. Her constant, loving, non-judgmental presence during the rest of Terry Jo's younger years was one of the rocks of Terry Jo's life. She was an example of endurance that Terry Jo would follow.

As Terry Jo tried to get into the swing of things, a problem emerged. As if Terry Jo didn't have enough of a burden to bear already, in all of the reunions she had even with those closest to her, there was still just a little awkwardness, a discomfort. Yes, Terry Jo was reserved and subdued, but there was more to it than that. No matter where she was, or with whom, there was always an elephant in the room. The elephant was the horrible experiences Terry Jo had gone through that no one talked about.

Since nobody had any idea how to deal with those experiences, there was an unspoken agreement among everyone never to discuss anything. Nobody knew what to say. Her well-meaning aunt and uncle decided that the best that could be done was for no one to mention what Terry Jo experienced. That was why no interviews were allowed, even though Terry Jo was the story of the year in Green Bay. Her aunt, uncle, and grandmother worked hard to spare her the stress, and try to give her as normal a life as possible. So everyone tried to live, almost literally, "as if nothing ever happened." And "everyone" included virtually an entire community.

Aunt Dot and Uncle Ralph told the parents of Terry Jo's friends never to bring up the *Bluebelle* tragedy, and these parents carefully instructed their children. When Terry Jo returned to sixth grade in De Pere in the spring of 1962, her teacher, a close family friend, also participated in the deception. Yet, everyone knew Terry Jo's story well; it had been covered in great detail by the local *Green Bay Press-Gazette* for weeks. What's more, Terry Jo knew that everyone knew (and they knew that she knew). To sense what this was like, all the reader has to do is think about how uncomfortable it is to be in a room when every single person is intentionally not talking about some big, ugly story that everyone knows about, concerning somebody who is also there, and that person knows that they know.

In Terry Jo's case, however, this awkward and uncomfortable conspiracy of silence went on for years! In fact, nineteen years would go by before Terry Jo would open up to anyone about what happened and how it had affected her. That included relatives, her closest friends, boyfriends, husbands, and, astonishingly, even a psychotherapist.

A full twenty-five years would go by before Terry Jo ever openly expressed anger at the loss of her family.

Terry Jo went from the unspeakable horror and terror of that night on the *Bluebelle*, to the long solitary ordeal on a flimsy piece of cork and webbing, to a third solitary ordeal that was to last far, far longer. Because of the conspiracy of silence, everyone's guard (including Terry Jo's) was always up, putting up barriers to close relationships. She would carry that elephant around with her for many years.

Terry Jo certainly had friends, and even close ones, but that sharing of one's most personal fears and troubles so essential between best friends in the early adolescent years was missing. There was too much of Terry Jo that was beyond the boundaries that had been established. Consequently, there were limits to how close anyone got to Terry Jo, or her to them. It was certain that Terry Jo herself did not really care to relive the horrors of her past, so she, too, had reason to avoid talking about it.

In order to spare her painful reminders of her previous life, Terry Jo's relatives also arranged to close down, empty, and sell the Duperrault family home near the bay – the cozy secure home with its thousands of memories, all of her mother's loving and artistic touches, her father's travel souvenirs and trophies, her brother's woodworking and art projects, her sister's doll collection – without Terry Jo ever returning there. She really had to begin a new life.

Terry Jo did insist, however, that she wanted to go back to get one thing: what she wanted to retrieve from her past life was not some comfortable reminder of innocence like a favorite Barbie doll (and she had many), not some familiar source of security like a favorite blanket or stuffed animal, not a special memento of the loving family that once was hers (and the house was full of them). She went back, instead, to get a reminder of the times when she felt *strong* – the Tarzan outfit that she wore when she bravely found her way alone through the pretend jungle.

Terry Jo knew full well that she faced a long, hard row, no matter how much the well-meaning people around her tried to shelter and protect her. She was wiser than her elders in many ways. Despite the love and protection of her aunt and uncle, and despite the especially authentic presence of Gammie's love, she knew that she would have to find her own way, alone. Where she was once grounded in innocence and security and had to pretend there was peril, she now inhabited an upside-down world born in peril and terror, and grounded in the loss of innocence and security.

Terry Jo was buoyed in facing her new life by believing that she must have survived for a reason. And that she had told the truth. The very first test she faced after the *Bluebelle*, her interview, she passed by telling the truth. Although she didn't know it at the time, the ordeal on the *Bluebelle* and on the sea had given her one thing that many adults do not have: she had integrity. Her simple, direct honesty would become a cornerstone of the rest of her life. Ask anyone who knew either the Terry Jo of that time or knows the Tere of today and they will emphatically agree. For the rest of her life she would hold onto the fact that she knew she had told the truth about what she saw on the *Bluebelle* that night, and that would give her strength.

But, how do you heal from the multiple traumas Terry Jo survived? In 1961 no one had yet heard of Post-Traumatic Stress

Disorder. But even not knowing about PTSD, Terry Jo would have at least have had to have met with a therapist to be assessed, and that was not yet part of the plan for her. If she had been evaluated, any psychologist would have picked up on the fact that she had paid a terrible emotional price. She did experience what later would be labeled one of the classic PTSD symptoms: survivor's guilt. She exhibited it by feeling guilty about not looking at her mother and brother after seeing them the first time, lying dead on the cabin floor. Although she has never been troubled by nightmares and flashbacks, which are two other classic PTSD symptoms, she developed two phobias since that night: blood and dark water. She cannot stand the sight of blood. The one situation where she toughs it out over blood is when she cares for injured animals, something she has done since she was a child. Love trumps many fears. She also loves the water and being on it and near it, but feels deeply anxious if the water is dark.

Many years later, she did show signs of two other classic PTSD symptoms: in the late '70s and early '80s, she went through a few years of low self-esteem and depression. But she blamed it on the bad marriage she was in at the time. She almost never exhibited the other classic symptoms of anger or flashes of temper; however, there was one night at her aunt's house some months after the *Bluebelle* when she was awakened by a scream. It took her a second to realize that her cousins were rough-housing in the next bedroom. She went in and let them have it. There was another time, twenty-five years after the *Bluebelle*, where she overheard a young colleague complaining about his parents getting divorced and how awful it was. Tere felt a rising fury. She nearly walked up to him and said, "I don't even *have* my parents!" But she controlled herself.

Terry Jo had experienced the instant horror of seeing two family members dead, the terror of the threatening captain, the fear of drowning in the sinking boat, and then the solitary ordeal of four days adrift alone and vulnerable where she began to ponder what had happened to her sister and her father, and to worry about being all alone in the world. She learned a week or so after being picked up about her sister's death. The fate of her father was uncertain for many days as far as officials were concerned; but for months and years, Terry Jo held out hope that he might somehow still be alive.

No one had ever seen anything close to what Terry Jo had gone through, and psychotherapy – even with children with more run-of-the-mill problems – was not highly developed at that time. Terry Jo needed to talk, but there was no one there to talk with. In 1961, there was only one therapist who worked with children in Green Bay. Even today, it would be hard to find a therapist trained in dealing with the kinds of multiple traumas that Terry Jo experienced. One would have to be adept in working with children from war zones who lost their families and who then had to hole up in terror for days with no food or water in a place where they could be killed at any minute.

We all know, of course, that children who are victims of war very often do not get much psychological care, though for different reasons than Terry Jo. We also know that the ravages can destroy these children for life. In Terry Jo's case, our current understanding that people need to talk to properly trained experts about horrors they have experienced was not widely accepted back then. The attempt to "protect" children who had been traumatized from any thing unsettling was far more pervasive. This was even more the case with Terry Jo. There was simply no precedent for how to treat Terry Jo and help her deal with the trauma she had endured.

In many ways Terry Jo might as well have been an alien from another planet, or a changeling who looked like Terry Jo but was really someone else who had taken her place, someone very different from the Terry Jo who left on that dream vacation worlds before. No one knew how to deal with her, except in the "let's-all-act-as-if-nothing-happened" mode. Terry Jo simply followed the lead of others and revealed little to nothing. Plus there was the squirm factor – the discomfort many people feel around those who have gone through horror, or are dying from some horrible incurable disease. The most understandable parallel might be how uncomfortable people can feel around a young woman who has been raped, even though it is clear she is thoroughly innocent. What do you say? In fact, Terry Jo's circumstance was, in many ways, similar to having been raped. She had her innocence wrenched from her in the most cruel and brutal of ways.

All of this meant that Terry Jo's healing would be mostly up to her, despite that fact that even the most mature and healthy adult would find it too much to do alone. Her journey toward healing would be long, lonely, and fraught with peril. There would be missteps. Though no longer on that flimsy raft, she was still alone and, in a way, adrift. She had no idea how long it would be before she might be rescued, or possibly land on solid ground on which to build a life.

Terry Jo did continue with some of her friendships even if there was never talk of her ordeal. Her best friend was a girl named

Pam, and next door to Pam lived a boy named Gregor. Pam's family became a second home for Terry Jo. They included Terry Jo in many of their activities and made it clear that she was welcome there any time. And in good, solid, mid-American fashion, they meant it. Terry Jo and Pam did typical, healthy early-adolescent things like talk about boys, hang out with friends, go to parties, and engage in mild hijinks like rolling some sleeping bags onto the back of their bicycles, peddling over to a gas station, and talking loudly about their long bike trip from Wyoming. Terry Jo loved Pam for helping her laugh. Pam worried that pretty Terry Jo would steal boys away from her.

Terry Jo's life was not completely lacking in friendships, or indeed love. The hearts of thousands went out to her; they just didn't know how to touch her.

One of the first things Terry Jo did might be seen as partly an act of escape, but it was also an act of seeking something new and positive. At the age of twelve, she decided on her own to change her name from "Terry Jo" to "Tere," though pronounced the same way. One day she simply informed her aunt, uncle, and everybody else that, from then on, she was to be known as Tere. To this day this is a legacy of the strength of Terry Jo's will. Terry Jo was gone forever, part of that other world that was also gone.

She made this change for several reasons. One is that the name "Terry Jo" was so linked to such horror that she wanted to get away from it. The name was also linked to her as a victim, and she wanted to get beyond that, too. The third reason was that she had gotten tired of repeatedly hearing about "brave little Terry Jo," as if people endlessly saying that would gradually push all of her demons away. It is ironic that she heard this so often while, at the same time, no one ever talked directly about the tragedy that required her to be so brave. She didn't need to hear that anymore; she knew she was brave. The fourth reason, as Tere will tell you, was that changing her name was something she could control. This proved to be the first big step in taking charge of who she was, rather than allowing the *Bluebelle* incident to forever define her.

After changing her name, Tere did not know how she would do it, but she set out alone to find better ground. She had no map, and no guide. She had learned that the adults around had no more of an idea than she did. Much of what she would do over the following years would involve both running away from her troubles while running toward something better at the same time. She embarked on a years-long experiment to try to discover who Tere would be.

By age sixteen, Tere had carried her elephant too long and was tired. She was also bristling under the restrictive protectiveness of her good-hearted aunt. Even though her grandmother remained her emotional ally, and her rock, there was some tension with her three male cousins because she got so much of their parents' attention. She also received material things because of an insurance settlement from boat owner Harold Pegg. He had been sued because it was determined that he had hired Harvey as a master when he did not have a master's license. The settlement was large enough to create a trust fund for Tere.

With her grandmother's blessing and strong support, and somewhat less enthusiastic support from "Mo" and "Unk," Tere decided she wanted to go to a private school to try to start over again, a place where she wouldn't have to carry the stigma of being the girl from the *Bluebelle* who went through stuff too terrible to talk about, a place where she didn't need to be a guarded person among guarded people. The trust fund, an increasing source of security, would pay for her schooling. She chose Ferry Hall, a private girls' school in Lake Forest, Illinois.

As it happened, she didn't have as much anonymity at Ferry Hall as she had hoped. Her senior Big Sister there turned out to be a student from Green Bay who knew about the famous Terry Jo Duperrault of the *Bluebelle*. Soon the rest of the school did, too. So she shared her dorm room with a roommate – and her elephant.

She became a close friend with her roommate, Janis, who invited her to visit her home in Indianapolis over the first winter holiday break. She met a boy there and proceeded to fall head over heels for him. When she was rebuffed – the rebuff including being told that she wasn't grown up enough yet – she was crushed. There was some teenage angst and dramatic heartache in this, of course – it was Tere's first hard-hitting, love-at-first-sight romance after all. Her heartbreaker told Tere that the 1967 Bobby Vee song, *Come Back When You Grow Up*, captured it all. But there was so much more than angst and teenage breakup for Tere: she felt kicked in the stomach, not just by a breakup but by a reminder of how alone she was. She was surprised by how hard she took it. For the first time in years – perhaps for the very first time ever – she felt truly overwhelmed by all she had lost. It all hit her at once. It was too much to bear, and she finally broke down. She wept more than she ever had, and was too broken up to function.

Tere returned to the comparative security and comfort of her aunt and uncle's home in De Pere, reconnected with some friends (including her best friend, Pam, and the neighbor boy, Gregor), and took some time off. Her aunt and uncle finally arranged for her to see a psychotherapist for help. Tere went to see him several times. She recalls that they talked about her emotional problems, adjusting to school, and problems with relationships, but (incredibly) they never talked about what happened on the *Bluebelle*. So a psychotherapist, no less, sidestepped the challenge of, and the need for, trying to get to the root of her problems.

This episode foreshadowed what would become a pattern in Tere's life: seeking, finding, and then losing a relationship. Broken hearts are, of course, part of the emotional obstacle course of a normal adolescence. As a normal, healthy teenager, she had yearnings. In Tere's case, however, the yearnings were deeper because, as psychologists might point out, she had lost so much, and she was still looking for her lost father, subconsciously if not consciously. As her emotional breakdown shows, her vulnerabilities were great. Needing somebody so much, she was vulnerable to being deeply hurt by their loss.

After returning to the Green Bay area and to her aunt and uncle, Tere returned to high school in East De Pere. She also reconnected with Gregor and they officially became girlfriend and boyfriend. Tere felt a special bond with Gregor because, a couple of years earlier, he had lost his father.

When Tere graduated from East De Pere High School, she remembered her father's challenge to his children that "travel is the best education." She decided to go to college to study Spanish. She chose the University of Wisconsin-Stevens Point partly because she knew they had a travel-abroad program.

The summer after freshman year, the adventurous nineteen-year-old Tere was in Spain. While there she traveled a lot, but especially fell in love with the Spanish islands of Majorca and Minorca. She took the ferry to them many times. She loved the beaches and the clear, emerald-colored water.

Not finding what she was looking for in studying Spanish language and culture, Tere dropped out of college after the fall semester of her sophomore year. She realized there was something else she was searching for, but she wasn't sure what it was. She would have to keep experimenting.

Because she knew she wanted to help people heal, but she could not deal with blood, she decided she would try studying to be an X-ray technician. She got an apartment the next fall in Milwaukee and began a joint program between St. Michael's Hospital in Milwaukee and the University of Minnesota. After the fall semester she moved to Minneapolis to continue the program at the university. She soon realized this wasn't what she was looking for either, and besides she missed Gregor a great deal. So she packed up and abruptly left Minneapolis. She knew that Gregor had left Green Bay to go skiing in Colorado, but she didn't know where. She missed him so desperately that she drove there in her Volkswagen Beetle and cruised through ski resort parking lots for days on end looking for his car. After a week or so, she gave up and came home to Aunt Dot and Gammie. It is tempting to point out that the quest to find her missing boyfriend is a metaphor for the continuing need to find her lost father. But she also needed to find something as yet unknown to replace what she had lost.

No sooner had she reconnected with Gregor back in Green

Bay than he got his draft notice. It was 1971. Vietnam. Once he got the notice, the two of them rushed off on a political-romantic-escapist-adventurous dash to Canada so he could avoid the draft. Canadian authorities at the border, however, wouldn't let them in. So they returned and Gregor dutifully reported to the draft board, ending up in the Army. This turned out to be a respite for Tere for, big-hearted as she was, she realized that she had been becoming more and more obligated to Gregor because he had lost his father, not because their relationship had other potential.

Later in the summer of 1971 Tere was at a 4th of July party with some friends. There she met a kind, attractive, and charismatic young man named John Satrazemis. Again, in that same pattern, she fell fast and hard for him; so hard and so fast that she married him three weeks later. Tere also liked John's four brothers very much, and they her, and almost instantly felt like she had a new family. Tere and John lived both in Florida, where John's brothers shared a house, and in Wisconsin. Their daughter, Brooke, was born in June 1974, but they divorced only a few months later. John, a good man in many ways, had proven not to be mature enough for the long-term responsibilities of marriage and fatherhood. And he had admitted that he was a less than faithful husband.

Even though her marriage had failed, Tere felt thoroughly embraced and welcomed by John's family. So she packed up her things, loaded baby Brooke into the car, and headed off alone to Florida to stay with John's four brothers. She was beginning to feel that she had to be a responsible adult now and she could not simply go back home this time to her Aunt Dot and Gammie. She also was exhibiting something else that was becoming another pattern in her life: heading to the sea in times of trouble.

It didn't take very long before the other pattern returned. A handsome young man named Spencer Hill was living with John's brothers in Florida. Spencer was nothing if not quick to (as Tere put it) "put the move on" her, and Tere was nothing if not quick to fall yet again. Soon she and Spencer had hooked up, baby and all. They and baby Brooke lived in a room in the brothers' house for a while, then, in another romantic-adventurous move that only young lovers can sustain, in 1975 the three of them moved into a tent in Naples, Florida, living in romantic poverty right next to the rich and famous.

That year Spencer joined the Army. In early 1976 Tere got pregnant. But Spencer, the romantic charmer, was not built from the kind of responsible stuff that makes for a solid marriage and a great parent. Even though Tere saw this pretty clearly, she felt trapped by her pregnancy, and she didn't want to have another child with no father. She knew too well how hard that could be. So she married Spencer in 1976 and had daughter Blaire that year. She vowed that she would work hard at being a good wife and mother. And besides, once again she was near the sea because they were stationed at Fort Bragg, North Carolina.

Now an Army wife married to a man planning an Army career, Tere had son Brian in 1978. That same year her beloved Gammie died, another devastating loss that Tere had to deal with and which once again forced her to face being so alone.

In 1979 Tere and her husband, three young kids in tow, were transferred to Germany, the front lines of the Cold War. Even though Tere remained unhappy in her marriage, and her husband was becoming colder and more distant (and he would later to be found to have a drug problem), she stayed out of obligation to her kids and to the idea of family. She tried harder to be a good wife and mother.

As part of setting up arrangements for medical care for Army families after arriving in Germany, a remarkable thing happened. It began ordinarily enough. While arranging to set up pediatric care for her children, Tere had filled out a routine questionnaire full of questions about family background, medical history, her children's vaccinations, the usual questions. To the question, "Are your parents living?" Tere, as she had done on other questionnaires over the years, simply checked "No." When the pediatrician, who would become her children's doctor, looked over the questionnaire in the routine parent-intake interview, he saw that question and the subsequent answer, then looked up and asked a simple, routine, obvious question:

"How did they die?"

A simple question that was simply profound. Tere had never been asked. So she answered.

Tere briefly said they had been killed, together, along with her brother and sister – all four of them, her world – on a sailboat a long time ago when she was young. The doctor's jaw dropped. She didn't go into much detail because the pediatrician interrupted and told her he wanted her to talk to his psychiatrist colleague. So, after nineteen long years of keeping so much of herself out of sight, Tere sat down and began to tell her story for the very first time. Slowly, very slowly, this began to change things. She had never before shared all of who she was. It was a new and unfamiliar experience. But the more she talked, the lighter that elephant began to feel, despite having to deal with a lot of pain as old issues kept so long in the dark began to come into the light. Ironically, it was around the same time that she was tracked down by a reporter from the *Green Bay Press-Gazette*, and an interview with her appeared in the paper. It was a big, front-page story. Everybody remembered Terry Jo and the *Bluebelle*.

Her journey and struggles were far from over. It would take years. But she finally had changed course and taken another step in the healing process. She would face more peril. She left Germany with her three small children and headed back to the United States. But she didn't go to Green Bay this time. She went to another place where she knew she would be welcome. She flew to Kansas where her old, good friend Pam now lived with her husband and baby. She was one of a number of people who loved Tere very deeply, and absolutely never failed to be there for her.

After catching her breath and taking stock, she filed for divorce from her husband who had failed to contact her.

She once again packed up her children and was on the move again, on her own again. She headed back for the familiar warmth and security of her Aunt Dot. Aunt Dot had not seen the children for some time, and this was the real beginning of their close relationship with their "Grandma," and one that would give them added security in the coming years. And Tere wanted that for her kids.

In the next few years Tere would go back to school, this time at the University of Wisconsin-Green Bay.

After a few years, another man would come into her life – a charming man, in fact. He seemed kind and interested in her children and she married him, but eventually he took advantage of her trusting nature and her need to be with someone. Tere prefers not to mention the name of this man, whose presence in her life she considers better forgotten. She discovered a well-concealed dark side that threatened her kids. She ran with her children one last time. But regardless of what else would happen, she knew she would get through it.

She had made some bad decisions, and some necessary ones. Yet she had given life. She had a family of three children who would prove to be remarkable people in their own right. She was strong for them. She loved and was loved by many. She had safe places: her aunt's home, her friend Pam's home, her first husband's family. She had touched many people, and not all because of the *Bluebelle*. Even though she had experienced failed relationships, she never had a failed friendship.

Despite having had to do so much on her own after the *Bluebelle* and having had her idyllic childhood wrenched away, she hadn't forgotten the lessons she learned from that world. She remembered what her parents, her grandmother, her aunt, and her uncle had taught her about love and family and the adventure called life; she remembered her multi-talented mother and her love of beauty; her dedicated father and his love of adventure (and, yes, she had traveled!); her brother and sister with all of the potential they represented; she remembered what neighbors had taught her about looking out for each other, about a work ethic from the rugged people of Green Bay.

She had moved many times on her own, taking first herself, then one, two, and three children with her.

Once she had children, she always put them first. "My mom taught my brother and sister and me to survive in every way," said Tere's eldest daughter, Brooke Satrazemis. "Thanks to her teaching and her love – and her amazing example – we all feel we can survive anything."

Whatever happened from here on out, she had a family; she had people to love, and to love her back. She had struggled mightily for years. But she was back home. And life had taught her much, not the least about what she was made of. She would get a good job and be greatly respected by her colleagues for her ethical approach to work, her kindness and support toward her colleagues, her dedication to the mission of caring for the natural world, and her good old-fashioned Green Bay work ethic.

And she had finally begun to tell her story. She had every reason to be consumed by anger, bitterness, and self-pity. But she wasn't. She could be excused had she found escape in drugs. But she didn't. She could have complained about her lousy lot in life. She never did. She had every reason to mistrust people, but she didn't. In the mid-1980s she would meet her co-author and they would begin talking about finishing the job of telling her amazing story.

Interview with Tere's daughter, Blaire, in 1999:
Question: "What do you think of your mom?"
Answer: "My Mom? She is my hero."

(Blaire became choked up as she gave her answer, gazing lovingly at her mom and displaying a broad smile.)

AFTERWORD

by Tere Fassbender

In 1990, I was working for the Wisconsin Department of Natural Resources, a job I had had since 1986. I was living in De Pere at the time. Our Water Resources staff was having a meeting that was to be moderated by the supervisor from Water Regulation and Zoning.

He walked into the room, flannel shirt, suspenders, blue jeans, work boots, greasy black hair, a beard, and a mustache long enough to drag in his soup. My first impression: "Who is this greaseball?"

Time passed and I never saw or thought of him. Then I applied for a job with Water Regulation and Zoning, a position responsible for wetlands and shoreline protection. Who was on the opposite side of the table interviewing me but the "greaseball." I must have interviewed well because I was given the job. I was a Water Management Specialist, assigned to protect our state's navigable waterways, working out of the Marinette DNR office. I loved my job and traveled the Northeastern region. This was a great way to get to know the lakes and rivers and, just like when I was a kid, I loved being outdoors on my own, sometimes even in risky conditions in remote areas.

That is how I came to know my boss, Ronald Fassbender. Many coworkers were fearful of him, as he had a scruffy appearance, a somewhat rough-edged manner, and a gruff raspy voice a little like Kris Kristofferson – one you could cut wood with. He looked and acted like a mountain man. In fact, I learned later that he *was* a mountain man – a re-enactor, that is. He was one of those guys who liked to camp out in the boonies and wear smelly, wet furs and call it fun. Women were especially cautious of Ron. I don't know why because I never had that fear, but only came to respect him and learn from him once I started getting to know him. Ron always was concerned for his staff, and they were his priority. He was very good at his job, no matter what his appearance. I learned that Ron was real and so comfortable with himself that he didn't need to try to impress anybody.

During this time I was having trouble with my marriage because my third husband had really pulled the wool over my eyes. He was not the kind and charming man I thought he was, but a manipulator who had successfully hidden the fact that he was a pedophile all during our courtship and marriage. Being the trusting person I am, and someone who always likes to think the best of people, I had not wanted to believe what my teenage daughters were telling me – about how he gave them the creeps – and I didn't want to believe it when he was charged with child molestation for an incident in town. He never molested my own kids, thank God, but they had been complaining more and more about his creepy and inappropriate behavior. In the beginning I was defending him and my children were acting out as a result. I thought it was mostly teenage rebellion, like I had gone through. Looking back, I do not blame them. I should have been more aware, more protective, and more trusting of my own children. Defending my husband and refusing to see what was happening caused my kids severe problems at the time, since they believed I wasn't being there for them. And I had always been there for my kids. They had been the center of my life ever since I had them. I think, in fact, that having them to take care of kept me doing something meaningful and helped me get through the very hard years after losing my family on the *Bluebelle*. My kids also helped me hold it together during all of the running I did for so many years. I guess I couldn't accept that my third choice for a husband hadn't been a good one, and that my third marriage wasn't going to work out either. I believed very deeply in marriage and in family, and I needed a partner in life.

I confided in Ron about the problems I was having, and he was supportive and understanding. He took extra time to meet with me and helped me sort through my job and family situations. He was very good in dealing with people problems.

I was so thankful for my job. I had moved to Oshkosh as the Water Management Specialist. My job was my haven where I could get away from my marriage problems. I had entered into my third marriage out of one of my strongest – and weakest – inclinations: being very trusting. I buried myself in my work and, for the most part, it kept me sane.

Ron and I became very good friends. I would tell him my problems and he would tell me his. In 1995, to get away from my now ex-husband, who had just been released from prison for felony child sexual abuse, I decided to leave the DNR and move to Wilmington, North Carolina. My in-laws from my first marriage lived there and said we could stay with them until we knew it was safe for me and my kids to return to Wisconsin.

Even though my first marriage had failed, too, I always had a wonderful relationship with my first husband's family, especially his brothers, and they were always there when I needed them. My first husband was not a bad person either; it is just that we were young and not right for each other. But I had been adopted like a daughter and sister by his family. That family, like many other wonderful people over the years, reached out to me. I owe them more than I could ever repay.

My son, Brian, found a job right away, as did my oldest daughter, Brooke, but my youngest daughter, Blaire, was lonesome for Wisconsin so she flew back to live with Grandpa and Grandma Scheer, the uncle and aunt who had adopted me. I found some work but was not happy, realizing I missed my best friend, Ron, so very much. We wrote letters and spoke on the phone daily. He flew to North Carolina for a brief visit. And, just like that, we realized we were in love.

Ron returned to Wisconsin, to his job and to a failing marriage. I stayed in Wilmington for another month to think about everything, and then decided I really wanted to be with him. I came back to Wisconsin and got my job back with the DNR. I felt so fortunate to again be doing the work I loved.

Ron and I have been together since Thanksgiving of 1995. Because I had always wanted to prove once and for all that I had told the truth about the *Bluebelle*, I agreed in 1999 to have a sodium amytal interview. Proving that I told the truth about what happened was most important to me, but the session also was used to see if we could uncover anything more about what really happened that night on the *Bluebelle*. I know that the psychiatrist was interested in whether I had repressed anything. I never felt afraid to confront the possibility that there might have been something I didn't remember because it was too terrible; I knew I had already remembered some pretty terrible things. When the psychiatrist decided that I hadn't repressed anything, and assured me that I had told the truth, I felt a new level of peace in my life, another step in healing.

In 2001 Ron and I retired from the DNR and decided we loved Kewaunee, Wisconsin, a small community located on the shores of Lake Michigan. We bought a house and are living the retired life there.

Of course I love being near the water and take as many walks along the shoreline as I can. It is a wonderful feeling but at times melancholy as I can hear the waves that sometimes remind me of my time on the ocean and of my family from so long ago. I feel closer to them there. While there is a melancholy feeling, it is also soothing; all in all, a sweet sadness. It is a place where my loyal little dog, Angel, and I can just be free and think.

My family has been very important to me. My children were raised as grandchildren to Dotty and Ralph Scheer, my aunt and uncle. We lost "Unk" in 1997, but he was Grandpa to my kids. A terrible loss to all of us. It was sad that my daughter, Blaire, did not have Grandpa at her wedding in 1999. But we gained a wonderful son-in-law, Jake.

My son, Brian, and his wife, Robbi, gave us our first grand child. I saw Alison born and I cried. She was such a miracle. Life is a miracle. I guess I have a special appreciation for that. Alison has spent lots of time with us and we are so proud of her.

Brooke, my oldest daughter, works in the movie industry

and recently moved from Austin, Texas, to Chicago. She loves the big city. We see her more often than when she lived in Austin.

Did I say how proud I am of my great kids?

In 2005 our first grandson, Wesley, was born. Alison has always loved her brother but they sure can get into scuffles. We have Wesley with us at times, but not as often as "Ali butt."

My beloved Aunt Dot, who was there for me always, died in the spring of 2008. She was very ill for six months and just kept getting worse and worse. I was with her as much as possible while she was in the hospital. It hurt to see her in so much pain. We all miss her, my kids especially, since she was always Grandma to them. She loved me and did her very best to protect me after the *Bluebelle*. Even though she kept me from truly dealing with the tragedy, she always gave me a safe place. Taking me in when she already had three sons was not easy, I am sure. As the years have gone by, I have appreciated what she did more and more.

Blaire and Jake gave us our second grandson, Arthur, born on September 5, 2009. He is such a happy little guy.

So you can see, after struggling for so many years, I now am in a very good place in my life. I count my blessings and am grateful for all the love and good health that I share with my family and friends.

The year of 2009 has been so good as I have reconnected with some very dear old friends.

My roommate from Ferry Hall, Janis, contacted me in April 2009. She was another steady friend who blessed my life. Her health was not good so I drove to Cicero, Indiana, for a few days to visit her. It was so wonderful to see my old friend. I left feeling so awful for her, but so thankful for my good health. We talked almost daily. On July 4 I received a call from Janis' husband who told me that she had died. I was in shock, thinking he was joking. I miss Janis but know she is in a better place and no longer suffering. Life is so often a matter of losses balanced by blessings.

In June, I heard from another old friend: my best friend, Pam, from my school days after the *Bluebelle* was visiting her sister in Green Bay. Pam has always been there, too, ready to welcome me any time for any reason. I went to visit her; we hadn't seen each other for years. We had fun reminiscing about the mischief we used to get into. As a bonus I got to see her father, Jack. In the years after the *Bluebelle*, he and his late wife, Mary Beth, had given me a second home I could always go to – and I was at their house a lot. Seeing Pam and her father was quite an event. I am so happy to have these people who have been a large part of my life back in my life.

I had lost track of my dear friend, Richard Logan. The last time I saw him he was very ill. Then I could not find him in the phone book and thought, perhaps, he had gone to greener pastures. But it turns out he had moved to Minneapolis with his wife, Carol, to be near their granddaughters and for medical treatment. We got back in touch in September, and I was thrilled to know that Dick was alive and well.

So we rekindled our friendship and wound up writing this book together.

I am grateful to Dick, as he has helped me through many rough spots. And now he is helping me to finally get over my tragedy. The elephant I carried for so long on my shoulders suddenly is no longer there.

My most recent rekindled friendship is with my long lost pen pal, Jean-Jacques, who lives near Paris. Jean-Jacques and I became pen pals as a result of the *Bluebelle* tragedy. He was one of hundreds who wrote me, asking to be a pen pal. The difference was that the two of us stayed in touch for many years. Jean-Jacques even visited us in 1968, and we wrote for many years after that. He stayed the summer with us at my aunt and uncle's home on Old Plank Road in De Pere. I think he had a crush on me.

I also thought something had happened to Jean-Jacques as I could not find him. So I looked on Facebook and there he was, just as I remembered him but with white hair instead of brown. It amazes me that so many people have come into my life for various reasons, and that there is so much love. I feel very loved and probably wouldn't be here otherwise.

What I want to stress to all who read this book is never give up, always have hope, and try to look on the bright side of things. Be positive, be trusting, and try to go with the flow; have compassion, give of yourself to those in need, and be loving and kind. I believe that what you give comes back to you.

Editor's note: Tere Fassbender was named Employee of the Year for the State of Wisconsin DNR in 1993. It was but one reflection of the kind of person that she had managed to become – and of the kind of person she always was.

EPILOGUE

Legacy One

On September 5, 2009, Tere's daughter, Blaire, the daughter who calls her mom her hero, gave birth to a son. She named him Arthur, after Tere's father who was never found but who has never been forgotten.

Many years before, Tere had given her son the name Brian after her lost brother, and Tere's cousin and an aunt and uncle named their daughters Jean René, after Tere's mother and younger sister.

Legacy Two

"IO[1], Miami report MC-1385 of 8 February 1962:
RECOMMENDATIONS

"... That consideration be given to amending the specifications for buoyant apparatus, life floats and life rafts (46 CFR 160.010, 160.018 and 160.027), to require that the body of such lifesaving equipment be painted or otherwise colored international orange.

"... That consideration be given to amending the vessel inspection regulations to require that the body of buoyant apparatus, life rafts and life floats used on board vessels or artificial islands and fixed structures on the outer continental shelf, be painted or otherwise colored international orange."

The above recommendations appear at the very end of the Coast Guard report on the *Bluebelle* case. They were duly adopted by the Coast Guard and have been in force now for decades. It is not generally known that the widespread use of international orange that we now take for granted is due to the ordeal of a brave young girl from Green Bay alone and almost invisible on the high seas on a tiny white raft. Since that change was made, untold numbers of others who would have been lost at sea have been found.

---

[1] "IO" is Coast Guard shorthand for "Investigating Officer"

BIBLIOGRAPHY

Information in this book was gleaned from many sources, some of which have been lost over the years since the author began compiling the material that eventually became this book. Among the sources are:

Extensive interviews with Tere Duperrault Fassbender.

Article by James Buchanan in *Argosy* magazine, *The Five Puzzles of the Death of Capt. Julian A Harvey*. March 1962.

Article by Robert Barber, *Miami Herald Sunday Magazine*, Miami, Florida. Nov. 28, 1971.

Article by Ruth Reynolds, *Reading Eagle Magazine*, Reading, Pennsylvania. June 23, 1963.

Articles by Michael Blecha, *Green Bay Press-Gazette*, Green Bay, Wisconsin. 1994 and 1999.

Article in *Life* magazine, *The Bluebelle Mystery*. Dec. 1, 1961.

Article in *Time* magazine, *The Sea: The Bluebelle's Last Voyage*. Dec. 1, 1961.

Broward County Library, Fort Lauderdale, Florida.

Broward County Sheriff's Department, Fort Lauderdale, Florida.

Brown County Library, Local History Section, Green Bay, Wisconsin.

Cofrin Library Reference Department, University of Wisconsin-Green Bay, Green Bay, Wisconsin.

Court record of Alachua County, Florida, 1945.

Court record of Dade County, Florida, 1958, 1959.

Court record of Hillsborough County, Florida, 1943.

Dade County, Florida, Sheriff's Department

Discovery Channel-Canada, Tere Duperrault documentary coverage. 2005.

Fort Lauderdale Police Department, Fort Lauderdale, Florida.

Green Bay Press-Gazette articles, photographs, Green Bay, Wisconsin.

Interview with Coast Guard officer Ernest Murdock, 1999.

Interview with Coast Guard officer Robert Barber, 1992.

Journals kept by Tere Duperrault Fassbender.

Miami-Dade Public Library

Miami Police Department

NASA

National Oceanographic and Atmospheric Administration weather records, November 1961.

Research and interviews by Ben Funk, Associated Press reporter, Miami.

Research and interviews by Gene Miller, reporter, *Miami Herald.*

Transcripts and records of U.S. Coast Guard inquiries, testimony and interviews regarding the *Bluebelle* case.

U.S. Coast Guard summary of *Bluebelle* case report.

U.S. Department of the Air Force

Weather records, U.S. Coast Guard office, Seventh District, Miami.

Web site of the 329th Bomb Group, U.S. 8th Air Force.

YouTube (film of Julian Harvey ditching the B-24)

INDEX